The Official
Driver Theory Test
Trucks and Buses
(Inc. Step 1 and 2 of
Driver CPC)
Questions and
Answers

Published by Prometric Ireland Limited under licence from the Road Safety Authority.

© 2017 Údarás Um Shábháilteacht Ar Bhóithre / Road Safety Authority

June 2017 Edition

ISBN 978-1-9997202-5-4

Prometric
La Touche House
Custom House Dock
IFSC
Dublin 1
DO1 R5P3
IRELAND

Foreword

As a learner driver, it is important that you have all the information you need to drive safely on our roads. Before you drive a Bus or Truck on public roads or in public places you must have a learner permit or a driving licence for the vehicle you want to drive. In most cases you must also pass a driver theory test to show that you understand what you must do to drive safely. The questions in the Truck and Bus driver theory tests, which are all in this book, are designed to test your knowledge and also to make you think about the different situations you will come across as a driver. If you wish to become a professional Truck or Bus Driver, you must also complete the mandatory Certificate in Professional Competence process (Driver CPC). This book contains questions from the Bus and Truck theory tests (Including Stage 1 of Driver CPC) as well as the case studies for Driver CPC - CPC Case Study theory test (Stage 2 of Driver CPC).

By studying the learning material and passing the Bus and/or Truck theory test you will have taken an important first step to becoming a safe driver. To be a professional driver you must also take the second step of passing the CPC Case study test. In order to be a safe & socially responsible driver, it is essential that you apply this knowledge and understanding whenever you are driving.

Learning to drive needs your time and patience, and the best way to learn is to take driving lessons from an approved driving instructor and get as much practice as you can

Finally, remember that driving should be enjoyable, and we wish you many years of safe driving.

Introduction and how to obtain a driving licence

Section 1: Trucks and Buses (Inc. Step 1 and 2 of Driver CPC)

Section 2: Case Studies

Introduction

To drive a motor vehicle on the public road in Ireland, you must hold a driving licence or a learner permit that covers the particular category of vehicle you plan to drive. For licensing purposes, there are fourteen categories of vehicle, identified by code letters – for example a Truck is Category C, a bus is Category D.

○ To obtain a learner permit, you must pass a driver theory test – that is what this book is about.

○ To obtain a full driving licence, you must first hold a learner permit, and develop your ability to drive the vehicle in a safe and socially responsible way, you must then pass a practical driving test.

With a learner permit, a number of restrictions apply, the most important of which is that you must be accompanied at all times by the holder of a full driving licence.

Who must take the driver theory test?

Before you can apply for your first learner permit in any driving licence category, you must have passed a driver theory test that relates to that category, and you must submit the driver theory test certificate to the licensing authority within two years of passing the test.

There are four different driver theory tests; which one you take depends on the category of vehicle you are planning to drive. This book covers all questions for the Truck and Bus driver theory tests, and different parts of the book are relevant to each test, as shown below.

If you wish to become a professional Truck or Bus Driver or drive a truck under the age of 21 years or bus under the age of 24 years then, you must also complete the mandatory Certificate in Professional Competence process (Driver CPC). This book contains case studies for the completion of the Driver CPC- CPC Case Study theory test. The table below also shows what parts of the book you should study to sit a CPC Case Study test.

Important: You must hold a full Category B Driving licence before you can book a driver theory test for a truck or bus theory test.

Category of vehicle you intend to drive		Parts of this book you need to study for driver theory test	Parts of this book you need to study to complete Driver CPC Case Study Test
C	Truck	Parts 1	Part 2
CE	Truck with trailer	Parts 1	Part 2
C1	Small truck	Parts 1	Part 2
C1E	Small truck and trailer	Parts 1	Part 2
D	Bus	Parts 1	Part 2
DE	Bus with trailer	Parts 1	Part 2
D1	Minibus	Parts 1	Part 2

Note that you do not have to pass the same theory test more than once. For example, if you pass the theory test for category C and obtain a learner permit for category C1, and you subsequently wish to obtain a learner permit for category CE, you are not required to take another driver theory test, provided you still have a valid learner permit or driving licence for category C.

In addition if you take and pass your Bus theory test now you can then choose to add the truck category at anytime in the following two years by sitting a shorter theory test of just 40 questions. These theory tests are known as either a Bus Module theory test or a Truck Module theory test

Preparing for the driver theory test

You should use this book and/or The Official Driver Theory Test Truck and Bus Questions and Answers CD-ROM as well as the Rules of the Road to prepare for the driver theory test. This book contains questions that you will be asked in your Truck and/or Bus driver theory tests, along with the correct answer and a brief explanation. Should you wish to become a professional driver of a truck or bus, this book also contains case studies for the CPC Case Study Theory Test that you will need.

If you spend sufficient time and effort preparing for your test, you should not find it difficult, and you should pass. More importantly, the knowledge you gain in preparing for the test will help to make you a better safe and socially responsible driver.

About the questions and answers in this book

In this book, you are presented with a question, the correct answer and an explanation (contained in the blue text box) as to why the answer is correct. Some questions may show a graphic which requires interpretation. For example:

What does this sign mean?
Crosswinds.

ABMW0099R

This sign gives advance warning that there may be crosswinds ahead. Crosswinds can affect the stability of your vehicle on the road.

In the test, you will be asked 100 questions and to pass you must answer at least 74 correctly. The questions will be taken from those set out in this book – you will not get a question that is not in the book.

In the test, each question you are asked is accompanied by four possible answers. Only one of these answers is correct, and you are required to identify it. The test is computerised and you will get a chance to practice before the test, so that you are familiar with the format.

Preparing for the CPC Case Study theory test

To prepare for your Truck or Bus CPC Case Study Theory Test you should study the following publications;

- This book-The Official Driver Theory Test Truck and Bus Questions and Answers plus CPC Case Studies or The Official Driver Theory Test CD-ROM Truck and Bus Questions and Answers plus CPC Case Studies
- The Rules of the Road
- Driving Goods Vehicles-The Official Driver Standards Agency (DSA) UK Guide

Or if you are doing the Bus Theory Test

• Driving Buses and Coaches-The Official Driver Standards Agency (DSA) UK Guide

In addition, the RSA have approved Driver CPC Training Centres which will help you in passing the Driver CPC Tests. A list of all RSA approved training centres is available on www.rsa.ie

The CPC Case Studies are short scenarios that describe various situations a bus or truck driver might face. There are 3 case studies with 15 questions in each case study (45 in total). To pass, you must correctly answer 28 of the 45 questions. You must answer correctly at least 5 questions on each case study.

Applying for a driver theory test

When you feel that you are well-enough prepared, apply to the Official Driver Theory Testing Service in one of the following ways:

Online:	www.theorytest.ie.
By telephone:	For an English language test call: 1890 606 106 For an Irish language test call: 1890 606 806
By post:	Complete an application form (obtainable from The National Driver Licensing Service (NDLS) or online from: www.theorytest.ie) and post it to: The Driver Theory Testing Service, PO Box 15, Dundalk, Co. Louth. When applying, please specify any special needs or language requirements that you have, so that appropriate arrangements may be made.

When booking a test, please have to hand credit/debit card details and your PSC Number.

Information on where and when theory tests may be taken can be obtained by contacting the Driver Theory Testing Service as above.

How to Obtain a Category C or D Driving Licence
Category C & D Licencing Process for Non-Professional Drivers

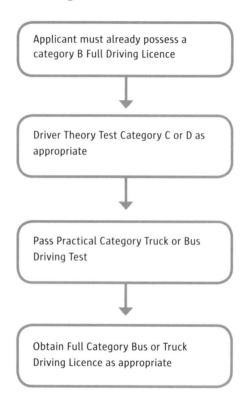

Applicant must already possess a category B Full Driving Licence

↓

Driver Theory Test Category C or D as appropriate

↓

Pass Practical Category Truck or Bus Driving Test

↓

Obtain Full Category Bus or Truck Driving Licence as appropriate

Minimum Age Requirements

- You must be a min. of 21 years of age to drive a Category C licence (truck) for **non-professional use.**
- You must be a min. of 24 years of age to drive a Category D (bus) for **non-professional use.**

However you may obtain a driving licence at the lower ages set out below:

- You must be a minimum of 18 years of age to apply for a first time Category C Driving licence with a CPC qualification to **drive professionally.**
- You must be a minimum of 21 years of age to apply for a first time Category D Driving licence with a CPC qualification to **drive professionally.**

How to Obtain a Category C or D Driving Licence
Category C & D Licencing Process for Professional Drivers (Min)

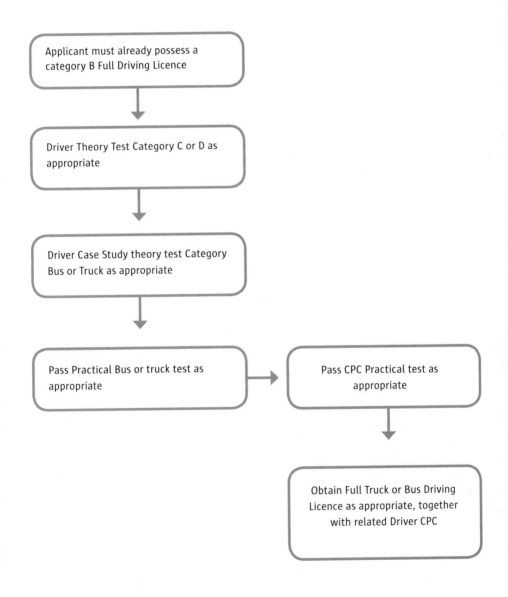

Applicant must already possess a category B Full Driving Licence

Driver Theory Test Category C or D as appropriate

Driver Case Study theory test Category Bus or Truck as appropriate

Pass Practical Bus or truck test as appropriate

Pass CPC Practical test as appropriate

Obtain Full Truck or Bus Driving Licence as appropriate, together with related Driver CPC

Trucks and buses
Legal matters

1

2

Rules of the Road

How many penalty points collected in 36 months will result in a driving ban?
CPC1106A

12 Points.

This is part of the penalty point system under Irish law. You will be banned from driving if you collect 12 points in a 36 month period.

If a fixed charge notice is received, the fine must be paid within how many days to avoid additional penalty?
CPC1107A

28 Days.

This is the fixed charge system under Irish law. This gives you 28 days to pay the fixed charge. Failure to pay will increase the charge by 50% (if you pay within the next 28 days).

A fixed charge notice contains all of the following information EXCEPT
when to appear in court.
CPC1108

This is Irish law as set by Road Traffic Act 1961 - 2005 (Fixed Charge Offences) Rules 2006. Usually there would be no court appearance necessary providing the fixed charge is paid in time.

If 12 or more penalty points are built up in a 36 month period, how many months is the driver banned from driving?
CPC1109

6 months.

This is Irish law as set by Road Traffic Rules 2006. Note - If you are banned from driving you must submit your driving licence to the National Driver Licence Service within 14 days.

When a driver is banned from driving, within how many days must the licence be handed in?
CPC1110A

14 Days.

A driver has to hand in their driving licence within 14 days - this is Irish law regarding driving bans.

ABMW0033R

What do these signs together mean?
Pedestrianised street ahead - traffic not allowed except during times shown.

This sign tells you that there is a pedestrian area ahead and that traffic is not allowed except during the times stated on the information plate.

ABMW0034

What does this sign mean?
Maximum permitted weight is 3 tonnes.

This sign tells you that that you must not enter this area if your vehicle is over the stated weight limit.

ABMW0037A

What does this sign mean?
Maximum permitted height of vehicle is the figure indicated.

This sign tells you that you must not enter this area if your vehicle exceeds the indicated height.

ABMW0038

What does this sign mean?
Parking of vehicles exceeding the weight shown is not allowed.

This sign tells you that you must not park in this area if your vehicle is over the weight limit indicated.

ABMW0039

What does this sign mean?
No overtaking.

This sign tells you that overtaking is prohibited in this area because it is dangerous to do so.

ABMW0040R

What do these signs together mean?
Only buses, cyclists and taxis are allowed to use the lane during the hours indicated.

This sign tells you there is a with-flow bus lane ahead – that is, one where the buses move in the same direction as the traffic to their right. The information plate tells the times when the bus lane is in operation. Only buses, taxis and cyclists may use the bus lane during those hours.

ABMW0041R

What does this sign mean?
With flow' bus and cycle lane ahead on left.

This sign tells you there is a with-flow bus lane ahead to the left. Only buses, taxis and cyclists may use the bus lane during the stated operational hours.

ABMW0042R

What does this sign mean?
With flow' bus and cycle lane on left.

This sign indicates a with-flow bus lane ahead. Only buses, taxis and cyclists may use the bus lane during the stated operational hours.

What does this sign mean?
Bus and cycle lane ahead on right.

ABMW0043R

This sign tells you that there is a bus lane ahead to the right. Only buses, taxis and cyclists may use the bus lane during the stated operational hours.

What does this sign mean?
Contra flow' bus lane ahead.

ABMW0045R

This sign tells you that you must drive on the left and not use the contra-flow bus lane ahead day or night. A contraflow bus lane is one where the buses are going in the opposite direction to the traffic on their right.

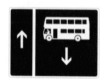

What does this sign mean?
Contra flow' bus lane ahead.

ABMW0046

This sign tells you that you must drive on the left and not use the contra-flow bus lane ahead day or night. A contra-flow bus lane is one where the buses are going in the opposite direction to the traffic on their right.

What does this sign mean?
Tram lane on right.

ABMW0050RA

This sign tells you there is a tram lane ahead to the right. Be aware that there might be pedestrians in the area and crossing the road.

What does this sign mean?
ABMW0078

Restricted headroom up ahead.

This sign gives advance warning that you are approaching an area of restricted headroom, such as a low bridge.

What does this sign mean?
ABMW0079

Overhead electric cables.

This sign gives advance warning of electric cables overhead. Drivers with a high load should be particularly careful.

What does this sign mean?
ABMW0099R

Crosswinds.

This sign gives advance warning that there may be crosswinds ahead. Crosswinds can affect the stability of your vehicle on the road.

What does this sign mean?
ABMW0106R

Tramway crossing ahead.

This sign gives pedestrians advance warning of a tram crossing where they should look both ways before crossing the road.

Where must a driver not park? ABMW0189R

Where there is a continuous white line along the centre of the road.

It is an offence to park at the side of a road that has a single or double continuous white line along its centre. Parking on such a road could create an obstruction and may cause inconvenience or danger to other road users.

For what distance before a zebra crossing is parking prohibited? ABMW0190R

15 metres.

It is an offence to park 15 metres before or 5 metres beyond a pedestrian crossing. Parking in this manner may restrict the zone of vision of drivers approaching the crossing and endanger pedestrians.

Within what distance of a junction is parking prohibited? ABMW0191R

5 metres.

It is an offence to park within 5 metres of a road junction unless parking spaces are clearly marked. Parking in that area may restrict the zone of vision of drivers approaching the junction and may cause an obstruction to large vehicles wishing to turn.

When may a driver park a vehicle in a loading bay? ABMW0192R

When the driver is the driver of a goods vehicle and is loading or unloading.

Loading bays are provided to enable goods vehicles to load or unload goods, up to a maximum of 30 minutes. Only goods vehicles are permitted to use loading bays.

Is a driver permitted to park at an entrance to a property? ABMW0193R

Yes, with the property owner's consent.

You may park across the entrance to a property only with the owner's consent. Parking across an entrance may cause inconvenience and danger to persons entering or leaving the property.

When is parking permitted on a footpath?
ABMW0194R
It is never permitted to park on a footpath.

It is always an offence to park on a footpath. Where a vehicle is parked on a footpath, pedestrians may have to step onto the road to go around the vehicle and so place themselves in danger.

When is double parking permitted?
ABMW0195R
Double parking is never permitted.

Double parking is never permitted. Parking is never permitted where it might interfere in any way with the normal flow of traffic or obstruct or endanger other road users.

When is parking permitted at a taxi rank?
ABMW0196R
Parking at a taxi rank is prohibited.

Stopping or parking within an area marked as a taxi rank is prohibited as this may obstruct taxis entering or leaving the rank.

1
2

When is parking permitted at a sharp bend?
ABMW0197R
Parking is never permitted at a sharp bend.

Parking is never permitted where it might interfere in any way with the normal flow of traffic or obstruct or endanger other road users – for example, by forcing other drivers into the path of oncoming traffic.

When is parking permitted on the brow of a hill?
ABMW0198R
Parking on the brow of a hill is never allowed.

Parking on the brow of a hill or on a humpbacked bridge is prohibited. Parking in such a place may restrict the zone of vision of drivers approaching the hill and force them into the path of oncoming traffic.

When are lighting up hours?
ABMW0207R

From just after dusk to just before dawn.

Lighting up hours are defined as the period of time during which drivers should turn on dipped headlights in order to be seen. This period normally starts half an hour after sunset and ends half an hour before sunrise.

What lights should a vehicle show at dusk?
ABMW0208R

Dipped headlights.

Drivers need to see and be seen during all periods of low light levels – for example, at dusk and dawn and in some bad weather conditions. At times of low light, you should turn on dipped headlights. The Road Safety Authority recommends that motorcyclists and drivers turn on their dipped headlights or daytime running lights during daylight hours.

What do rumble strips warn a driver of?
ABMW0209R

A danger immediately ahead or to the side.

Rumble strips are a patterning in the surface of the roadway that causes a rumbling sound when you drive over them. The purpose of them is to warn you to of a potential danger ahead or to the side.

What is the purpose of traffic calming measures?
ABMW0210R

To slow down traffic in the vicinity.

The purpose of traffic calming measures is to slow down fast-moving traffic to a speed more suitable for the area they are entering. These measures are usually found in rural areas on the entry points to towns or villages.

When may a trailer be towed on a public road without a rear number plate?
ABMW0211R

Never, a number plate must always be displayed.

The law requires all motorised vehicles to display a rear number plate that is clean and legible.

When may you pass another vehicle on the left-hand side? ABMW0212R
When the vehicle in front is signalling to turn right or in slow moving lanes of traffic.

Normally you must overtake on the right. There are, however, circumstances where you may overtake on the left – for example, when the vehicle has moved out and signalled to turn right.

Who can use a signed cycle track accompanied by a continuous white line on the left-hand side? ABMW0213R
Cyclists and users of motorised wheelchairs.

A cycle track is for the use of cyclists and motorised wheelchairs only. No other vehicles may cross into or over a mandatory cycle track unless this is necessary in order to leave or enter a side road or a property adjacent to the cycle track.

What traffic may drive along on a cycle lane accompanied by a continuous white line? ABMW0214R
Cyclists and motorised wheelchairs.

A cycle track is for the use of cyclists and motorised wheelchairs. No other vehicles may cross into or over a mandatory cycle track unless this is necessary in order to leave a side road or a property adjacent to the cycle track.

What traffic may drive along on a cycle lane accompanied by a broken white line? ABMW0215R
Cyclists and users of motorised wheelchairs.

A cycle track is for the use of cyclists and motorised wheelchairs only. No other vehicles may cross into or over a mandatory cycle track unless this is necessary in order to leave or enter a side road or a property adjacent to the cycle track.

When must drivers stop at a railway level crossing controlled by lights and barriers? ABMW0216R
When the red lights start to flash.

You are legally required to stop at a level crossing when the red lights start to flash and the warning bells sound. You must wait for all barriers to open fully before proceeding.

1
2

At a level crossing with unattended gates, what should a driver do?
Open both gates before proceeding to cross. ABMW0217R

At a level crossing with unattended gates a driver must stop, look for trains and listen for the sound of a horn or approaching trains. If it is safe, open both gates, complete the crossing and then close both gates.

What lights indicate a zebra crossing? ABMW0218R
Flashing amber beacons.

A zebra crossing is indicated by amber flashing beacons on poles and black and white stripes on the road. You must stop for pedestrians on the crossing and for those about to cross.

What do flashing amber arrows indicate? ABMW0219R
Drivers should proceed in the direction indicated.

When you meet a flashing amber arrow, you should proceed in the direction indicated provided it is safe to do so. Large flashing amber arrows can be found at roadworks on dual carriageways and motorways.

What do temporary traffic lights at road works mean? ABMW0220R
A driver must comply with the lights at all times.

You must comply with any temporary traffic lights used to control vehicle movements at or near road works. It is an offence not to obey these lights.

When do temporary speed limits apply at roadworks? ABMW0221R
For the duration of the roadworks.

Temporary speed limits at road works apply for a limited period of time. When road works are completed, normal speed limits apply.

What does this sign mean?

ABMW1A

No entry to goods vehicles with five axles or more.

This sign tells you that heavy goods vehicles with five or more axles are not permitted to enter this road.

What does this sign mean?

ABMW2

Tram lane on left.

This sign tells you there e is a tram lane on the left. Be aware that there might be pedestrians in the area and crossing the road.

1
2

What is the number of penalty points on payment of a fine for a licensed bus driver travelling at 100Km/h on a national road?

RSA01004

Three Penalty points

The number of penalty points recorded under the fixed penalty points scheme for driving a bus at 100Km/h on a national road where the limit is 80km/h is set at three. This may increase to five penalty points following a court appearance.

What should a driver be aware of before moving off?

D13A

Persons attempting to get off the bus.

Before moving off from a bus stop, drivers should always make sure all passengers boarding and leaving the bus have done so. Pay particular attention to older passengers who might be slow when boarding or leaving.

Licensing

How frequently must a vehicle be submitted for certificate of roadworthiness test? CD0002
Annually.

All commercial vehicles – that is, goods vehicles, buses carrying more than 8 passengers, and ambulances – must be tested for roadworthiness (commercial vehicle test or CVT) when they are one year old and annually after that.

What learner permit drivers in categories C, C1, D and D1 are required to be accompanied by the holder of a full licence? CD0003R
All.

If you hold a learner permit for category C, C1, D or D1, you must be accompanied and supervised at all times while driving by someone who holds a current full driving licence for the same category of vehicle.

What category of licence must a driver hold in order to drive a vehicle with a Maximum Authorised Mass (M.A.M) of 7,500kgs with seating for no more than 8 passengers? C0001AA
Category C1, C1E, C or CE.

To drive a rigid vehicle with a design gross vehicle weight of between 3,500kg and 7,500kg, you must hold a category C1 licence. Above 7,500kg DGVW, you need a category C licence.

What is the Maximum Authorised Mass (M.A.M) of a vehicle that the holder of a category C1 licence may drive? C0002AA
7,500kgs.

To drive a rigid vehicle with a design gross vehicle weight of between 3,500kg and 7,500kg, you must hold a category C1 licence. Above 7,500kg DGVW, you need a category C licence.

Is the holder of a category C1 licence entitled to tow a trailer?
Yes, up to 750kgs Maximum Authorised Mass (M.A.M). C0007RA

If you hold a full category C1 licence, you may tow a trailer with a design gross vehicle weight of 750kg or less. However, if you hold a category C1 learner permit, you may not tow a trailer.

Is the holder of a category C learner permit entitled to tow a trailer when driving a category C vehicle? C0008RA
No, the holder of a category C learner permit must not tow a trailer.

If you hold a learner permit for category B, C1, C, D1 or D, you may not tow a trailer. A full licence holder in one of these categories may tow a trailer with a design gross vehicle weight of 750kg or less.

Is the holder of a category C licence entitled to tow a trailer when driving a category C vehicle? C0009RA
Yes, provided the trailer does not exceed 750kgs Maximum Authorised Mass (M.A.M).

If you hold a full category C licence, you may tow a trailer with a design gross vehicle weight of 750kg or less. However, if you hold a category C learner permit, you may not tow a trailer.

What is the maximum number of passengers that can be carried by the holder of a Category C or C1 licence? C0010R
8 passengers.

If you hold a category C or C1 licence, you are permitted to drive vehicles with seating for up to 8 passengers plus the driver.

What does the term Maximum Authorised Mass (MAM) refer to?
The maximum weight for which a vehicle is designed. C0012A

Goods vehicles normally have a plate fitted showing the maximum gross weight, the maximum axle weights, and the train weight. These maximum weights must be complied with when the vehicle is used on the road.

25

What does this information sign indicate about the load when displayed on a truck or trailer? C0013RA
Bio Hazard

This sign indicates the type of material carried and the level of hazard associated with it.

Is the holder of a category D or D1 learner permit allowed to carry passengers for hire or reward while driving a bus? D0003R
No.

The holder of a learner permit driving a car, van, bus or coach must not carry any passengers for payment of any kind.

Must the holder of a category D learner permit who holds a category D1 full licence display L plates on a bus or coach while taking driving lessons? D0005R
Yes, at all times.

The holder of a learner permit (in every category except A1, A and M) must always display proper L-plates on the front and rear of the vehicle they are driving.

Must the holder of a category D learner permit who already holds a category D1 full licence be accompanied by the holder of a category D licence when driving a bus or coach? D0006R
Yes, at all times.

A learner permit holder in category D must always be accompanied and supervised by the holder of a full licence in that category.

Is a driver who holds a full category D licence restricted to automatic transmission (code 78) permitted to drive a conventional manual bus or coach on that licence? D0007R
No.

If you pass your driving test in a vehicle equipped with automatic transmission, a code 78 is noted in the restrictions column of your full licence. This restricts you to driving only vehicles with automatic transmission. If you subsequently wish to drive a manual vehicle in that category, you must obtain a new learner permit and comply with the regulations pertaining to learner permits, including L-plates and accompanying driver.

A Category C1 licence is required to drive which of the following? C1315
A vehicle with a Maximum Authorised Mass (MAM) of 7,500 kg or less.

A category C1 licence holder may drive a vehicle with a maximum authorised mass not exceeding 7,500 kg and seating for up to 8 passengers.

A Category C1E licence is required to drive which of the following? C1316A
A vehicle in category C1 towing a trailer, where the combined Maximum Authorised Mass (MAM) is 12,000 kg or less.

A Category C1E licence holder may drive a Category C1 vehicle towing a trailer where the maximum authorised mass of the combined vehicles does not exceed 12,000 kg.

A Category CE licence is required to drive which of the following?
A vehicle in category C, which is towing a trailer that has a Maximum Authorised Mass (MAM) greater than 750 kg and includes an articulated unit. C1317

A Category CE licence holder may drive a Category C vehicle towing a trailer where the maximum authorised mass of the combined vehicles is greater than 750 kg.

To apply for a truck learner permit an individual must satisfy which of the following conditions? C1318
Normally resident in Ireland.

To apply for a truck learner permit you must be at least 18 years of age and normally resident in Ireland.

To apply for a Category C learner permit an individual must already hold a licence in which of the following categories?   C1319
B.

To apply for a Category C learner permit you must already hold a Category B licence.

To apply for a Category C1 learner permit an individual must already hold a licence in which of the following categories?   C1320
B.

To apply for a Category C1 learner permit you must already hold a Category B licence.

A Category D1 licence permits the holder to drive a vehicle which can carry how many passengers (apart from the driver)?   D1316
9-16 passengers.

A Category D1 licence holder may drive a vehicle with seating for 9 to 16 passengers, apart from the driver.

A Category D licence permits the holder to drive a vehicle which can carry how many passengers (apart from the driver)?   D1317
More than 8 passengers.

A Category D licence holder may drive a vehicle with seating for more than 8 passengers, apart from the driver.

A Category (DE) licence is required to drive which of the following?
A vehicle that carries more than 8 passengers towing a trailer which has a Maximum Authorised Mass (MAM) greater than 750kg.   D1319

A Category DE licence holder may drive a vehicle that carries more than 8 passengers combined with a trailer if the maximum authorised mass of the trailer is greater than 750 kg.

To apply for a bus learner permit an individual must satisfy which of the following conditions?   D1320
Normally resident in Ireland.

To apply for a bus learner permit you must be at least 21 years of age and normally resident in Ireland.

To apply for a Category D learner permit an individual must already hold a licence in which of the following categories?   D1321
B.

To apply for a Category D learner permit you must already hold a Category B licence.

To apply for a Category D1 learner permit an individual must already hold a licence in which of the following categories?   D1322
B.

To apply for a Category D1 learner permit you must already hold a Category B licence.

To apply for a Category (DE) learner permit an individual must already hold a licence in which of the following categories?   D1323
D.

To apply for a Category DE learner permit you must already hold a Category D licence.

To apply for a Category (D1E) learner permit an individual must already hold a licence in which of the following categories?   D1324
D1.

To apply for a Category D1E learner permit you must already hold a Category D1 licence.

Who is required to hold a road passenger transport operator's licence?
A person or firm with a business involved in transporting persons by road for reward.   D0009R

In order to operate a business involved in the transport of persons for reward by road, the operator must hold a road passenger transport operator's licence. For the full period of validity of the licence, the operator must employ a transport manager who holds a certificate of professional competence in road passenger transport.

What is the minimum age at which a CPC driver can drive a 53-seater bus or coach?
21 years

To avoid breaching the law it is essential to know and comply with all the licensing requirements. Whilst the general minimum age for driving a large bus or coach is 24 yrs. a driver may obtain a driving license for Category D at the age of 21 if he/she also holds a Drivers Certificate of Professional Competence (CPC).

What is the minimum age at which a driver can drive a 14-seat bus?
21 years

To avoid breaching the law it is essential to know and comply with all the licensing requirements. The minimum age for driving a mini-bus is 21 years of age.

What is the minimum amount of periodic refresher training that the holder of a bus drivers CPC must do, each year, to maintain their qualification?
Seven hours

Once a bus driver obtains his/ her Drivers CPC they must then complete periodic refresher training to maintain it. In Ireland, periodic refresher training consists of a course of 35 hours broken down into 5 annual modules each lasting a minimum of 7 hours.

A bus on the road required to display a valid Commercial Vehicle Roadworthiness Test (CVRT) disc when it is older than?
1 year

All commercial vehicles must be tested when they are over one year old and annually after that. Commercial Vehicle Testing is one component of the preventative measures we need to have safer vehicles on our roads. The Commercial Vehicle Roadworthiness Test (CVRT) is a roadworthiness test for all commercial vehicles over one year old. The CVRT confirms that a vehicle satisfies basic safety standards on the day the test is carried out. It tests what is accessible and visible.

What rules apply to towing a trailer for a Category D1 learner permit holder?
The holder may not tow a trailer.

Category D1 drivers may not tow a trailer without holding a full license in the category.

What is a legal requirement for any organised bus trip carrying children?
Must have appropriate and fit for purpose safety belts or restraint systems.   RSA01008

Important Regulations concerning children and safety belts on buses come into effect on the 31 October 2011. The Road Traffic (Restraint Systems in Organised Transport of Children) Regulations (Statutory Instrument No. 367 of 2011) make it a legal requirement that all buses involved in the organised transport of children must be fitted with appropriate and fit for purpose safety belts or restraint systems.

Which of the following is a condition of the 12 day rule for international coach journey?
The journey is a single trip.   RSA01009

Professional drivers can only work for 12 consecutive days if they follow the rules before during and after their international coach tour trip.

Which of the following is a minimum rest period option that an international coach tour driver must take before using the 12 day rule?
Take a rest period of 45 hours immediately before the journey.   RSA01010

Professional coach drivers can only work for 12 consecutive days if they follow the rules before during and after their international coach tour trip.

Which of the following is a requirement of the 12 day rule for international coach tour driving after 1st January, 2014?
If the driving time is between 10pm and 6am, you must have more than one driver, or you can't drive more than 3 hours without a break.   RSA01011

Future requirements After 1st January, 2014, there will be 2 additional requirements for coach drivers taking 12 day trips (1)You must have a digital tachograph fitted to your vehicle (2)If your driving time is between 22:00 and 06:00, you must have more than one driver, or you can't drive more than 3 hours without a break.

What operator is exempt from carrying a Road Haulage Operators Licence?
An operator that owns a category C type truck and uses it to transport own goods.   RSA01017

You need a Road Haulage Operator's Licence if you are carrying goods for hire or reward in a vehicle or combination of vehicles the maximum authorised weight of which is in excess of 3.5 (metric) tonnes.

Crime

Who is responsible for ensuring a vehicle is NOT transporting illegal immigrants?
CPC1188A
The driver.

You may face penalties if you bring illegal immigrants into the country in your vehicle, whether you know they are there or not.

After parking at a border crossing, who is responsible for checking that the vehicle has not been tampered with?
CPC1199A
The Driver

You should carry out all security and checks even more carefully when travelling abroad, especially if your vehicle has been unattended at any time when parked at a border crossing.

When should a driver search his/her vehicle?
CPC1202
Before a route and before starting a return route.

Carry out a security check before you drive your vehicle. Search your vehicle at the end of a route and before starting your return journey, to ensure that nothing has been concealed or left behind.

On an international journey, when should a driver check his/her vehicle?
At the appropriate times throughout the journey.
CPC1202A

Carry out a security check before you drive your vehicle. Search your vehicle at the end of a route and before starting your return journey, to ensure that nothing has been concealed or left behind.

When travelling abroad, what should drivers do if they find a suspicious item within or around the vehicle?
CPC1209AA
Arrange for the appropriate authorities to deal with the item.

If you find unattended luggage, you should contact the company and arrange for it to be removed as soon as possible.

LEGAL MATTERS » CRIME

Which of the following may assist a driver to avoid penalties for carrying illegal immigrants?

CPC1215A

Making use of vehicle checks provided by port operators.

It is best practice to operate an effective system to protect your vehicle against carrying illegal immigrants. An effective system is made up of three parts – vehicle security, vehicle checking and documentation. This includes vehicle checks provided by Ports.

What are the three parts of an effective system to protect the driver against carrying illegal immigrants?

CPC1220

Vehicle security, vehicle checking, and documentation.

It is best practice to operate an effective system to protect your vehicle against carrying illegal immigrants. An effective system is made up of three parts – vehicle security, vehicle checking and documentation.

Which of these is one of the most common causes of criminal damage to vehicles?

CPC1425

Missile throwing.

The most common forms of criminal damage are missile throwing, slashed seats, graffiti and broken windows.

Which area of a vehicle must be checked for unauthorised access?

CPC1437

Axle.

As well as checking the other areas, you must check the underside of the vehicle as illegal immigrants sometimes hide above the vehicle axle.

Speed Limits

What is the maximum permitted speed on a motorway of a single-decker bus or minibus (having passenger accommodation for more than 8 persons) and which is not designed to carry standing passengers?
100km/h.   D0060R

A single- or double-decker bus or coach that is not designed to carry standing passengers is subject to a general speed limit of 100km/h on motorways, unless a lower speed limit is in place.

What is the maximum permitted speed on a dual carriageway of a single-decker bus or minibus (having passenger accommodation for more than 8 persons) and which is not designed to carry standing passengers?
100km/h.   D0061R

A single- or double-decker bus or coach that is not designed to carry standing passengers is subject to a general speed limit of 100km/h on a dual carriageway, unless a lower speed limit is in place.

What is the maximum permitted speed on a national primary road of a single-decker bus or minibus (having passenger accommodation for more than 8 persons) and which is not designed to carry standing passenger?
80km/h.   D0062R

A single-decker bus or minibus that is not designed to carry standing passengers is subject to a general speed limit of 80km/h on national roads, and 100km/h on motorways and or dual carriageways, unless a lower speed limit is in place.

What is the maximum permitted speed on a motorway of a double-decker bus or minibus (having passenger accommodation for more than 8 persons) and which is not designed to carry standing passengers?
100km/h.   D0063R

A single- or double-decker bus or coach that is not designed to carry standing passengers is subject to a general speed limit of 100km/h on dual carriageways, unless a lower speed limit is in place.

What is the maximum permitted speed on a dual carriageway of a double-decker bus or minibus (having passenger accommodation for more than 8 persons) and which is not designed to carry standing passengers?
D0064R
100km/h.

A single- or double-decker bus or coach that is not designed to carry standing passengers is subject to a general speed limit of 100km/h on dual carriageways, unless a lower speed limit is in place.

What is the maximum permitted speed on a national primary road of a double-decker bus or minibus (having passenger accommodation for more than 8 persons) and which is not designed to carry standing passenger?
D0065R
80km/h.

A single-decker bus or minibus that is not designed to carry standing passengers is subject to a general speed limit of 80km/h on national roads, and 100km/h on motorways and dual carriageways, unless a lower speed limit is in place.

What is the maximum permitted speed on a motorway of a single-decker bus or minibus (having passenger accommodation for more than 8 persons) and which is designed to carry standing passengers?
D0066R
65km/h.

A single-decker bus or minibus that is designed to carry standing passengers is subject to a general speed limit of 65km/h on motorways, unless a lower speed limit is in place.

What is the maximum permitted speed on a dual carriageway of a single-decker bus or minibus (having passenger accommodation for more than 8 persons) which is designed to carry standing passengers?
D0067R
65km/h.

A single-decker bus or minibus that is designed to carry standing passengers is subject to a general speed limit of 65km/h on dual carriageways, unless a lower speed limit is in place.

What is the maximum permitted speed on a national primary road of a single-decker bus or minibus having passenger accommodation for more than 8 persons and which is designed to carry standing passengers?
65km/h. D0068R

A single-decker bus or minibus that is designed to carry standing passengers is subject to a general speed limit of 65km/h on national and primary roads, unless a lower speed limit is in place.

What is the maximum permitted speed limit on a motorway of a double-decker bus or minibus (having passenger accommodation for more than 8 persons) and which is designed to carry standing passengers?
65km/h. D0069R

A double-decker bus or minibus that is designed to carry standing passengers is subject to a general speed limit of 65km/h on motorways, unless a lower speed limit is in place.

What is the maximum permitted speed on a dual carriageway of a double-decker bus or minibus (having passenger accommodation for more than 8 persons) and which is designed to carry standing passengers?
65km/h. D0070R

A double-decker bus or minibus that is designed to carry standing passengers is subject to a general speed limit of 65km/h on motorways, unless a lower speed limit is in place.

What is the maximum permitted speed on a national primary road of a double-decker bus or minibus (having passenger accommodation for more than 8 persons) and which is designed to carry standing passengers?
65km/h. D0071R

A double-decker bus or minibus that is designed to carry standing passengers is subject to a general speed limit of 65km/h on motorways, unless a lower speed limit is in place.

What is the maximum permitted speed of a truck?
C1300
90 km/h.

A truck is subject to a maximum speed limit of 90 km/h. This applies to motorway driving only, unless a lower speed limit is in place. Trucks are subject to a general speed limit of 80 km/h.

What is the maximum permitted speed of a truck on a motorway?
C1301
90 km/h.

A truck is subject to a speed limit of 90 km/h on a motorway, unless a lower speed limit is in place.

What is the maximum permitted speed of a truck on a national primary road?
C1302
80 Km/h.

A truck is subject to a general speed limit of 80 km/h, unless a lower or higher speed limit is in place.

What is the maximum permitted speed of a truck on a dual carriageway?
80 Km/h.
C1303

A truck is subject to a general speed limit of 80 km/h, unless a lower or higher speed limit is in place.

What is the maximum permitted speed on a motorway of a goods vehicle with a Maximum Authorised Mass of more than 3,500kg?
C1304A
90 km/h.

Vehicles with a Maximum Authorised Mass above 3,500 kg are permitted to travel at 90km/h on motorways, and a general speed limit of 80 km/h on all other roads, unless a lower speed limit is in place.

What is the maximum permitted speed of a goods vehicle with a Maximum Authorised Mass (MAM) of 3,000kg? C1305
120 Km/h.

Vehicles with a Maximum Authorised Mass below 3,500 kg are subject to the speed limits which apply to cars and smaller vehicles, which is 120 km/h, unless a lower speed limit is in place.

What is the maximum permitted speed of a truck in a town/city (built-up) area? C1306
50 km/h.

Trucks, like all vehicles, are subject to a speed limit of 50 kilometres per hour in built-up areas (other than motorways or special speed limit zones).

What is the maximum permitted speed of a truck on a regional or local road? C1307
80 Km/h.

A truck is subject to a general speed limit of 80 km/h, unless a lower or higher speed limit is in place.

What is the maximum permissible speed of a car towing a trailer on national primary roads? ABMW0187
80 Km/h.

When towing a trailer on a national primary road, it is illegal to exceed 80 Km/h – exceeding this speed will make the vehicle unstable,

What is the maximum permissible speed of a car towing a trailer on a motorway? ABMW0188A
80 km/h.

When towing a trailer on a motorway it is illegal to exceed 80 Km/h – excessive speed may make such a vehicle unstable.

Driving hours and rest periods

EU regulations on driving hours were introduced to reduce the incidence of driver fatigue, which is a known risk factor in road collisions. If you drive a bus or truck, there are detailed regulations relating to the hours you may drive, and the breaks and rest periods you must take. The purpose of these rules is both to improve your working conditions and to contribute to road safety by reducing the risk of your becoming fatigued. The questions in this section are designed to check that you know and understand these regulations.

Driving Hours and Breaks Regulations

According to EU driver's hours regulations, a break is required for the driver after driving   CPC1098
four and a half hours.

This is EU law as set by Council Rules (EEC) 3820/85 and 561/2006.

Under EU drivers hours regulations, what is the minimum number of consecutive hours of daily rest a driver must take?   CPC1100
11 reduced to 9.

This is EU law as set by Council Rules (EEC) 3820/85 and 561/2006. It is also Irish law and helps make our roads safer.

After four and a half hours of driving, how long a break must a driver take?   CPC1290
45 minutes.

Under EU rules, after driving no more than 4.5 hours you must take a break of at least 45 minutes unless you take a rest period.

What is the maximum time a driver can drive between weekly rest periods?   CPC1291
56 hours.

There is a maximum weekly driving limit of 56 hours and you must take a weekly rest period after no more than six daily driving periods. You may drive up to 56 hours between weekly rest periods. Rules set under EU 561/2006.

Under EU driving hours regulations, what is the maximum hours that may be driven in a given week?   CPC1294
56 hours.

Under EU rules (EU 561/2006), the maximum weekly driving limit is 56 hours.

Under EU driving hours regulations, the shortest break that a driver can take in a driving period is
CPC1295
15 minutes.

Under EU and Irish law, your first break from driving must be at least 15 minutes.

Under EU drivers' hours regulations, a driver must take a break after how many hours driving?
CPC1385
4.5 hours.

EU rules state that all drivers must take an uninterrupted break of 45 minutes after four and a half hours of driving. You could face fines and lose your licence if you don't comply.

Under EU drivers' hours regulations, after driving for four and a half hours, a driver must take an uninterrupted break of
CPC1386
45 minutes.

You must take a break of at least 45 minutes after 4.5 hours of driving. It also helps make our roads safer.

Under EU drivers' hours regulations, a 'day' means a period of
CPC1387
24 hours.

Under EU rules, a day is defined as any 24-hour period beginning when you start driving after your last daily or weekly rest period.

What is the maximum number of hours that a driver can drive in a given week?
CD0007R
56 hours.

EU regulations specify that a driver can drive no more than 56 hours in a given week.

1
2

What is the maximum permitted number of driving hours in a two-week period?
CD0008

90 hours.

EU regulations specify that a driver can drive no more than 90 hours in a two-week period.

What is the minimum break time that should be taken for each break during or following a driving period?
CD0009R

15 minutes.

EU regulations specify that a driver must take a break of at least 15 minutes during or following a driving period.

What is the minimum break time which must be taken following a 4.5 hour driving period?
CD0010R

45 minutes.

EU regulations specify that a driver must take a break of at least 45 minutes after driving for 4.5 hours.

What is the maximum number of hours a driver may drive in week two, if 56 hours were worked in week one?
CD0011R

34 hours.

EU regulations specify that a driver can drive no more than 90 hours in a two-week period.

On how many days of the working week may a driver drive for more than 9 hours?
CD0012R

2 Days.

EU regulations on driving hours were introduced to reduce the incidence of driver fatigue, which is a known risk factor in road collisions. These regulations specify that a driver must not drive for more than 56 hours a week, with a maximum of 10 hours a day for two days, 9 hours a day for four days and at least one full rest day.

On how many days of the working week may a driver drive?
CD0013R

6 Days.

EU regulations on driving hours were introduced to reduce the incidence of driver fatigue, which is a known risk factor in road collisions. These regulations specify that a driver must not drive on more than six days in any week and must not exceed 56 driving hours in the week.

On three days of the week what can the minimum daily rest period be reduced to?
CD0014R

9 hours.

EU regulations on driving hours were introduced to reduce the incidence of driver fatigue, which is a known risk factor in road collisions. These regulations specify that a driver must take an 11-hour rest period within each 24-hour period. This may be reduced to 9 hours on a maximum of three days in a two-week period.

1

2

What is the normal minimum weekly rest period?
CD0015R

45 consecutive hours.

EU regulations on driving hours were introduced to reduce the incidence of driver fatigue, which is a known risk factor in road collisions. These regulations specify that a driver must normally take two rest periods, each of 45 consecutive hours, in a two-week period.

On a rest day, may a driver carry out other 'paid duties' apart from driving?
CD0016R

No. It is a rest day.

EU regulations on driving hours were introduced to reduce the incidence of driver fatigue, which is a known risk factor in road collisions. These regulations specify that a driver is not permitted to do any paid work on a rest day, driving or otherwise.

Tachograph

A driver did not use a tachograph chart on a new journey. Which of the following is the MOST severe penalty risk? CPC1112
Loss of licence and heavy fines.

This is EU law as set by Council Regulation (EEC) 3821/85 and SI No. 89 European Communities (Road Transport) (Recording Equipment) Regulation 2006.

A driver has driven a vehicle on a journey and has not used a tachograph. What is the MOST severe penalty risk? CPC115B
Loss of licence and heavy fines.

This is EU law as set by Council Regulation (EEC) 3821/85 and SI No. 89 European Communities (Road Transport) (Recording Equipment) Regulation 2006.

A device that records hours of driving, breaks and rest periods is a CPC1288
tachograph.

A tachograph is a measuring instrument that records hours of driving, breaks and rest periods as well as the distance you travel and speed you travelled at.

What does this tachograph symbol mean? CD0017R
Driving period.

Tachographs (recording devices) are required to be fitted to trucks over 3.5 tonnes and to buses with more than 9 seats. They record the driver's driving activity, rest periods, vehicle speed, distance travelled and other information. The driver should select the symbol that represents the activity they are engaged in – rest, driving or other work. The records must be retained for inspection by Enforcement Officers.

What does this tachograph symbol mean?
CD0018R
Period when the driver is available to work.

Tachographs (recording devices) are required to be fitted to trucks over 3.5 tonnes and to buses with more than 9 seats. They record the driver's driving activity, rest periods, vehicle speed, distance travelled and other information. The driver should select the symbol that represents the activity they are engaged in – rest, driving or other work. The records must be retained for inspection by Enforcement Officers.

What does this tachograph symbol mean?
CD0019R
Other work - that is, work other than actual driving.

Tachographs (recording devices) are required to be fitted to trucks over 3.5 tonnes and to buses with more than 9 seats. They record the driver's driving activity, rest periods, vehicle speed, distance travelled and other information. The driver should select the symbol that represents the activity they are engaged in – rest, driving or other work. The records must be retained for inspection by Enforcement Officers.

What does this tachograph symbol mean?
CD0020R
Rest period.

Tachographs (recording devices) are required to be fitted to trucks over 3.5 tonnes and to buses with more than 9 seats. They record the driver's driving activity, rest periods, vehicle speed, distance travelled and other information. The driver should select the symbol that represents the activity they are engaged in – rest, driving or other work. The records must be retained for inspection by Enforcement Officers.

Who is responsible for ensuring that a tachograph chart is properly completed and inserted into the tachograph?
CD0022R
The driver.

EU regulations require the driver to keep daily records. The driver is responsible for ensuring that the tachograph chart is properly completed and inserted into the tachograph.

What information is recorded on a tachograph chart? CD0023R
Driving time, vehicle speed and distance.

The tachograph chart records a driver's driving hours, vehicle speed, and distance covered. It is used to check that the driver takes at least the legal minimum amount of rest during the working day.

Which tachograph records must be retained by the driver? CD0025R
Records for the current day and the 28 calendar days immediately preceding that day

The tachograph chart records a driver's driving hours, vehicle speed, and distance covered. It is used to check that the driver takes at least the legal minimum amount of rest during the working day. The regulations require the driver to keep records for the current and the previous 28 days, and to produce them on demand.

When must a new tachograph chart be placed in a tachograph? CD0026R
At the start of each working day.

EU regulations require the driver to keep daily records. The driver is responsible for ensuring that the tachograph chart is properly completed and inserted into the tachograph at the start of each working day.

Who is responsible for making sure that a driver's card is properly CD0181R
inserted into the digital tachograph unit?
The driver of the vehicle.

Driver smart cards were introduced to prevent driving hours offences. The regulations require the driver to insert their driver smart card into the digital tachograph unit when taking charge of a vehicle.

What time and day denote the beginning of a week for tachograph purposes? CD0027R

00.00 hours on Monday.

The tachograph chart records a driver's driving hours, vehicle speed, and distance covered. It is used to check that the driver takes at least the legal minimum amount of rest and does not exceed the legal maximum driving hours in a day, week or fortnight. For tachograph purposes, the week starts at 00.00 hours on Monday and finishes at 24.00 hours on Sunday.

If two drivers are intending to use the same vehicle in a given day what should the first driver do? CD0029R

Remove their tachograph chart when they leave the vehicle and insert it again when they recommence driving the vehicle.

EU regulations require that if a vehicle is being used by more than one driver in a given day, each driver should use their own tachograph chart for that day.

1

2

If, in a given day, two drivers intend to use the same vehicle fitted with a digital tachograph, what should the first driver do? CD0180R

Remove their driver's card from the digital tachograph unit of the vehicle when they leave it.

EU regulations specify that if a vehicle is being driven by more than one driver in a given day, each driver must use their own driver's card in slot one of the digital tachograph unit while they are operating the vehicle and remove it when leaving the vehicle.

Driver Records and Driver Cards

Under what circumstances can a driver's rest period be taken in a parked vehicle? CD0031R
If the vehicle is fitted with a bunk.

Drivers are required to take a daily rest period of at least 11 hours. This can be broken down into one uninterrupted period of 3 hours and a second uninterrupted period of at least 9 hours. Drivers may take their rest periods in a parked vehicle only if the vehicle is fitted with a bunk.

What can a bus or truck driver do to stay alert on a long journey? CD0032
Wind down the window and reduce the temperature in the driver's compartment.

Fatigue is a known risk factor in road collisions. EU regulations specify legal minimums for rest periods so that drivers are able to drive their vehicles in a safe manner. During a journey, a driver should take planned rest breaks, avoid making the driving area too warm, and avoid eating large, heavy meals.

What in particular should a professional driver who works long hours be aware of? CD0033R
Fatigue affects alertness and ability to react.

Professional drivers must avail of regular adequate rest periods to avoid fatigue. EU regulations on driving hours specify legal minimum rest periods, and maximum driving hours in a day, week and fortnight.

What driver records must be produced by a driver to an enforcement officer at a roadside inspection? CD0185R
The driver's card.

Driving hours, rest periods and breaks are recorded by a tachograph, either digitally on the driver card or graphically on a tachograph chart. Drivers are legally required to carry records of activity for the preceding 28 days and to produce these records for inspection when requested by enforcement officers.

A driver is required to drive two or more vehicles fitted with digital tachographs at different times during their working day. One of the vehicles is used during a period which is exempt and 'out of scope' from driver's hours and tachograph requirements. What should the driver do?
Use the tachograph's manual input facility to record 'other work'.   CD0186R

Where a driver performs both 'in-scope' and 'out-of-scope' (exempt driving) in the same week, the out-of-scope driving can be recorded by manual entry on the digital tachograph unit.

A driver is working away from a vehicle and the driver's card is not inserted in the digital tachograph. What should the driver do?   CD0189R
Manually enter times and activities in the tachograph.

Driver smart cards were introduced to prevent driving hours offences. If at the start of the working day a driver is engaged in non-driving duties away from the vehicle, they should manually enter a record of the other work activities into the digital tachograph when they take the vehicle in charge.

1

2

How long may a driver continue to drive without a driver card if their card has been lost or stolen?   CD1300
15 days.

Driver smart cards were introduced to prevent driving hours offences. The regulations require the driver to insert their driver smart card into the digital tachograph unit when taking charge of a vehicle. If a card is lost or stolen the regulations require it be replaced promptly.

What should a driver do with a driver card that has malfunctioned?
Return it to the Road Safety Authority.   CD1301

Driver smart cards record personalised data about the driver and their driving activity, and play a central role in preventing driving hours offences. Malfunctioning cards should be returned to the Road Safety Authority so they can be disposed securely and analysed if necessary.

How often must the data on a driver card be downloaded? CD1302
Every 21 days.

Driver smart cards were introduced to prevent driving hours offences. The regulations require that the data on the cards be downloaded every 21 days.

Who should a professional driver notify if his tachograph card is lost or stolen? RSA01029
Gardaí and Road Safety Authority

For lost/stolen cards only: bring your application to a Gardaí station. The Gardaí must complete, sign and stamp the Gardaí Report on Section 1. If your digital tachograph card is lost, stolen, damaged, or malfunctioning, you should apply to the Road Safety Authority to have it replaced as soon as possible. If your digital tachograph card is damaged or malfunctioning, it must be returned to the Road Safety Authority with your application for a replacement.

Who is responsible for the long term storage of tachograph data after 21 days? RSA01030
Operator

Operators/Companies must keep a copy for at least one year of both driver tachograph data as well as those from Vehicle Units (or mass memory) and therefore regularly download.

Who should you notify if your tachograph card is damaged? RSA01031
Road Safety Authority

For damaged cards only: send your card to the RSA (with your application).

Technical
Matters

General

The body of a vehicle with air suspension may move quite a lot while parked due to
CPC1153
air being exhausted from the air bags.

Air suspension relies on an air supply. When the engine is not running, air leaks from the bags and the vehicle body can move in the direction of an emptying bag.

What does this symbol mean?
CD0070
Electrical cut-off switch.

For safety reasons, buses and some trucks are fitted with an electrical cut-off switch. This enables you to disconnect battery power from all the vehicle's systems. It is especially important to use this switch in the event of an incident where there is a fire or fuel spill.

What does a load-sensing valve do?
CD0071
Adjusts the brake pressure which is applied at the wheels.

A load-sensing valve regulates the pressure passing to the brakes, so that maximum pressure is available only when the vehicle is fully laden. As the load on the vehicle reduces, the valve automatically lowers the braking pressure.

What does 'road-friendly' suspension do?
CD0072R
Reduces the impact of a vehicle's weight on the road.

Road-friendly suspension, also known as air suspension, protects the load in a vehicle by reducing vibration. It can also reduce the damage to road surfaces and bridges caused by heavy loads.

What would be the likely effect of a defect in the power steering system?
It could make the steering seem heavy and stiff to turn.   CD0073

Power steering is a system that reduces the effort that a driver needs to turn the front wheels.
It generally consists of a fluid reservoir and a hydraulic pump powered by the engine. If the
pump malfunctions or the fluid level drops, steering the vehicle may become very difficult.

**What would indicate to the driver that there was a problem with the
power steering?**   CD0075
Inability to easily turn the steering wheel.

Power steering is a system that reduces the effort that a driver needs to turn the front wheels.
It generally consists of a fluid reservoir and a hydraulic pump powered by the engine. If the
pump malfunctions or the fluid level drops, steering the vehicle may become very difficult.

Mirrors

1

2

What effect can wet weather have on the vehicle's exterior mirrors?
It can distort the rear vision of the driver.   CD0083R

When you are driving in the rain, water droplets can adhere to the exterior mirrors and obscure
your view to the side and rear of the vehicle. If your vehicle has heated mirrors, turn them on to
clear them. Alternatively, stop periodically to clear them manually.

**When preparing to perform a manoeuvre, drivers should follow which of
the following activity sequences?**   CD1318
Mirror Check - Signal - Manoeuvre.

Drivers must always use the mirrors effectively before any manoeuvre. The Mirror Check-Signal-
Manoeuvre routine ensures that they look before they signal, signal before they act and act
sensibly based on what they see in the mirrors.

Drivers should check their nearside mirror every time they pass   CD1319
a parked vehicle.

Drivers should always have a good idea of what's happening to the rear, as well as in-front,
of the vehicle when performing a manoeuvre such as passing a parked vehicle.

When preparing to perform a manoeuvre, mirrors must FIRST be used before the manoeuvre. CD1320

Drivers must always use their mirrors effectively before any manoeuvre.

A driver must use their mirrors effectively before which of the following events? CD1321
Decreasing speed.

Drivers must use their mirrors effectively before a number of key manoeuvres, including increasing or decreasing speed.

1

2

Drivers should check their nearside mirror after they have CD1323
passed a cyclist.

Drivers must use their nearside mirror after a number of key events, including passing a cyclist or motorcyclist.

Drivers should check their nearside mirror after they have CD1324
passed a pedestrian standing close to the kerb.

Drivers must use their nearside mirror after a number of key events, including passing a pedestrian standing close to the kerb.

A driver sees a parked car some distance ahead. Preparing to move out, they check their offside mirror. The primary reason for this mirror use is to CD1325
check for a vehicle that may attempt to overtake from the rear.

The primary danger when moving out to pass a parked car is that someone may attempt to overtake you as you need to move out. Checking the offside mirror enables the driver to identify this risk.

Optimisation of Fuel Consumption

What should be done with the airlines of an uncoupled tractor unit?

They should be properly stowed away.

C0029R

When uncoupling a tractor unit from a trailer, the air-lines should be stowed safely, using the hooks or other facilities provided for the purpose on the tractor unit. If you don't do this, the lines can get damaged, for example by getting burned by the exhaust system or getting tangled up in the drive shaft.

Why should the fifth wheel drawing plate on an articulated truck be sufficiently greased?

To reduce wear.

C0030R

In order to prevent premature wear on the drawing plate and latching mechanism, the fifth wheel should be cleaned, inspected for damage and re-greased regularly. Keeping the fifth wheel well greased makes it easier to couple and uncouple a trailer, and also allows smoother articulation between the tractor and trailer when turning.

What should a driver check after driving a truck over rough or broken ground?
C0031R

That stones are not jammed between the rear twin wheels.

After driving a truck over rough ground, make sure that it has not picked up any rocks or debris between the rear twin wheels. You should also check this as part of your daily routine.

What is the purpose of a 'range-change' gearbox?
C0032R

It offers the driver a selection of high and low gears to suit the load being carried or the terrain.

A 'range-change' gearbox offers a wider range of gears than a standard gearbox. By offering the choice of high or low ratios, it effectively doubles the number of gears available, so that the driver can choose the most appropriate gear for the road and the load being carried.

1
2

What is the advantage of a two-speed axle?
C0033R

It doubles the number of gear ratios available to a driver.

A two-speed axle doubles the number of gear ratios available to the driver by offering a choice of two final drive ratios in the rear axle. The selection is made by operating an electrical switch.

What does an unloader valve do?
C0034R

It releases excess air pressure in the braking system.

An unloader valve prevents the build-up of excess pressure in the air tanks of a vehicle fitted with air brakes. The valve is fitted between the compressor and the air tanks. It opens and closes at pre-set pressures, and you will hear a change in the sound of the compressor as it operates.

When should a driver use a diff-lock on a truck?
CD0080R

When stuck on soft ground.

A driving axle is fitted with a differential, which allows the wheels on either side to rotate at different speeds, so that the vehicle can negotiate bends and corners. The purpose of a diff-lock is to cause the wheels to rotate at the same speed, and this is used when extra traction is required, for example if the vehicle is stuck in mud or snow. The diff-lock should be used only at low speed and should be disengaged as soon as possible.

When should a driver use a diff-lock in a truck?
CD0081R

When stuck on snow or ice.

A driving axle is fitted with a differential, which allows the wheels on either side to rotate at different speeds, so that the vehicle can negotiate bends and corners. The purpose of a diff-lock is to cause the wheels to rotate at the same speed, and this is used when extra traction is required, for example if the vehicle is stuck in mud or snow. The diff-lock should be used only at low speed and should be disengaged as soon as possible.

The diff-lock has been engaged to enable a truck to move off on a slippery road surface. When should the driver disengage it?
CD0082R

As soon as the truck is underway.

A driving axle is fitted with a differential, which allows the wheels on either side to rotate at different speeds, so that the vehicle can negotiate bends and corners. The purpose of a diff-lock is to cause the wheels to rotate at the same speed, and this is used when extra traction is required, for example if the vehicle is stuck in mud or snow. The diff-lock should be used only at low speed and should be disengaged as soon as possible.

An unloader valve is a device which is fitted to a
C1308

air brake system.

An unloader valve is a device fitted to air brake systems, pre-set to operate as sufficient pressure is achieved and allowing the excess to be released.

The purpose of airlines and 'suzie' lines are to
C1309

supply air and electricity from a vehicle to a trailer.

'Suzie' and air lines provide an air/electricity connection between the vehicle and the trailer.

The effect of a two-speed axle is to
C1310

double the number of ratios available to the driver.

A two-speed axle is a system whereby an electrical switch activates a mechanism in the rear axle that doubles the number of ratios available to the driver.

A driver is approaching a muddy surface. To assist traction they should engage the
C1311

diff-lock.

Engaging the diff-lock ensures that power is transmitted to all driven wheels. This aids traction on surfaces such as mud or snow.

What is the purpose of a diff-lock?
CD0079R

It locks up the differential to improve traction on soft ground.

A driving axle is fitted with a differential, which allows the wheels on either side to rotate at different speeds, so that the vehicle can negotiate bends and corners. The purpose of a diff-lock is to cause the wheels to rotate at the same speed, and this is used when extra traction is required, for example if the vehicle is stuck in mud or snow. The diff-lock should be used only at low speed and should be disengaged as soon as possible.

The technique of double declutching matches
CPC10017

engine speed to a lower gear.

Double declutching is way to engage and release the clutch when changing down in order to adjust engine revs to road speed. This reduces the load placed on the gearbox. This is rarely needed in modern vehicles.

What is the relationship between torque, power and fuel consumption?
As torque increases, power and fuel consumption increase.   CPC1005

The torque produced by an engine will vary at different engine speeds. If you can achieve optimum torque at low engine speed, you will use much less fuel compared to an engine running at maximum revolutions. Torque helps to achieve optimum engine efficiency.

Torque is transmitted from the engine and eventually to the wheels by the   CPC1007
gearbox and drive shaft.

Torque and power created by the engine are transferred to the wheels via the gearbox and drive shaft.

What is the primary function of the instrument in the picture above?
To help the driver decide what gear to use.   CPC1010

The rev counter (or tachometer) measures the engine speed. For best performance, you need to match vehicle and engine speed by selecting the correct gear. The rev counter helps you to select the proper gear for the engine speed.

Refer to the accompanying image. Which reading would indicate the most efficient use of engine power for a vehicle travelling at a moderately steady speed?
15   CPC1011

For a moderately steady vehicle speed you need the highest gear with the lowest engine rpm. 1500 rpm is the optimum for this speed, which reads as 15 on the rev counter. 500 rpm is too low to maintain engine function while 2500 rpm and above would cause undue engine wear.

Refer to the accompanying image. When the needle moves from 10 to 20, this indicates an increase in
engine power.   CPC1012

On a manual gearbox, lower numbers on the gearstick represent lower gearbox ratios.

When driving a vehicle with a fully automatic gearbox, how would the driver engage the 'kick down' facility to overtake a slow-moving vehicle?
CPC1015
Push the accelerator to the floor.

Some automatic gearboxes have a 'kick down' feature that allows you to engage a lower gear when you need rapid acceleration. To use this feature, press the accelerator to the floor.

While driving a vehicle fitted with a crash gear box, the driver when changing down briefly releases the clutch with the gear lever in the neutral position. This is
CPC1016
double declutching.

Double declutching is a way to engage and release the clutch when changing down in order to adjust engine revs to road speed. This reduces the load placed on the gearbox. This is rarely needed in modern vehicles.

Refer to the accompanying image. Which number represents the lowest gearbox ratio?
CPC1018
1.

On a manual gearbox, lower numbers on the gearstick represent lower gearbox ratios.

Refer to the accompanying image. Which number or letter refers to the highest gearbox ratio?
CPC1019
5

On a manual gearbox, higher numbers on the gearstick represent higher gearbox ratios.

Which of the following is generally TRUE regarding the relationship between fuel consumption and gearbox types?
CPC1057A
Vehicles with manual transmission generally use less fuel than vehicles with automatic transmission.

Drivers who are skilled in using manual transmissions change gears less frequently and stay in the most efficient gear possible. These techniques save considerable amounts of fuel.

Missing out intermediate gears while changing down can result in lower fuel consumption.

CPC1058

When a driver doesn't go through every gear while changing down, the engine revs less and uses less fuel.

The driver can use less fuel when accelerating by missing out intermediate gears.

CPC1059

When a driver doesn't use all the gears while changing up, the engine accelerates less and uses less fuel.

To save fuel, a driver can use the highest gear that doesn't make the engine struggle.

CPC1060

When using the highest gear, the engine turns less and so uses less fuel. If the engine begins to struggle, more fuel will be needed to keep it running.

When is the most fuel consumed while changing up in gear? While accelerating before selecting a gear.

CPC1061

Reduce the amount of time you spend accelerating when you can, as this is when you use the most fuel. As conditions allow, use the highest gear possible without making the engine struggle.

Which gear should be used to optimise fuel consumption? The highest gear possible without making the engine struggle.

CPC1067

As conditions allow, use the highest gear possible without making the engine struggle. This will reduce the amount of time you spend accelerating, which is when you use the most fuel.

What technique should be used when driving away? Pull away smoothly.

CPC1068

A driver should drive away smoothly for maximum safety and fuel efficiency.

To improve fuel economy, a driver should change down to the appropriate gear, but

CPC1072

change gears when speed has decreased.

When changing down you should wait until your vehicle speed decreases so as not to over-rev the engine, which would use more fuel and cause engine wear.

To maintain vehicle safety, what might a driver do when driving downhill?

CPC1078

Use a lower gear.

Using a lower gear when you can increases the braking effect of the engine. This makes the vehicle slower and more stable.

For the most efficient use of power and fuel, the driver of a vehicle with a full load should

CPC1079

accelerate slowly when starting off.

Rapid acceleration and over-revving the engine uses more fuel and causes wear on the engine. When starting off, regardless of load, you should accelerate smoothly.

1

2

What effect do heavy braking and rapid acceleration have on fuel consumption?

CPC1081

Both increase fuel consumption.

Rapid acceleration and heavy braking use more fuel. Heavy braking usually means you will need to accelerate afterwards to build up the vehicle momentum again.

On vehicles with cold-start or excess fuel devices, when should the driver push the device in?

CPC1085

Once the engine runs smoothly without it.

Pushing in the cold-start or excess fuel device once the engine runs smoothly, will save fuel.

keeping the vehicle at a consistent speed, cruise control can save fuel.

CPC1086

By keeping a steady vehicle speed, the engine runs more efficiently so cruise control may save fuel. Cruise control also allows the electronic control system to deliver the appropriate amount of fuel for every driving condition.

What can an increase in the average fuel consumption mean?
The vehicle needs servicing.

CPC1091

If you haven't changed your driving methods, or driving conditions haven't changed, an increase in fuel consumption usually means the vehicle needs servicing.

Engines powered by what type of fuel are usually the MOST fuel efficient?
Diesel fuel.

CPC1093

Diesel engines are usually more fuel efficient than petrol engines.

What type of engine oil can help to save fuel?
Synthetic oil.

CPC1094

Synthetic motor oil causes less engine drag than the other forms of oil listed. This means the engine wastes less power and saves more fuel in the process.

In normal driving, fuel can be saved by keeping the rev counter needle
lower than the speedometer needle.

CPC1096

When the rev counter reads lower than the speedometer, the engine is moving slower than the vehicle. This is best for fuel economy.

Compared to one with a petrol engine, a vehicle with a diesel engine can pull more weight at a
lower engine rpm.

CPC1391

Diesel engines give maximum power at minimal fuel consumption because they are high compression-ignition engines. The higher compression uses less fuel for ignition.

To save fuel, the driver should
use cruise control as much as possible.

CPC1402

Cruise control helps the electronic control system to deliver the right amount of fuel for any given situation. Only use a cruise control system when it is safe & appropriate to do so.

What is the function of the transmission system in a truck or bus? CD0088R
To transmit power from the engine to the wheels.

The transmission system of the engine is made up of the clutch, gearbox and driveshafts. Torque power is transmitted from the driveshaft of the engine to the road wheels via the clutch and gearbox to make the vehicle move.

What should a driver do to avoid excessive exhaust pollution from their vehicle? CD0168R
Have the vehicle serviced regularly.

You can reduce the amount of exhaust pollution created by your vehicle by reducing speed, avoiding severe braking and harsh acceleration, and having the vehicle serviced regularly.

How would a driver improve efficiency? CD0169R
Use gentle acceleration and make gear changes to maximize efficiency.

To improve fuel efficiency, save money and help the environment, you should reduce speed, brake and accelerate gently, and change gears efficiently, as recommended by the vehicle manufacturer.

1
2

How could a driver reduce exhaust pollution? CD0170R
Make sure that the engine is serviced regularly.

You can reduce the amount of exhaust pollution created by your vehicle by reducing speed, avoiding severe braking and harsh acceleration, and having the vehicle serviced regularly.

When driving a tipper truck and about to exit a quarry, what should a driver ensure? C4
That there are no stones lodged between the twin-wheels.

When driving a HGV, you must make sure that the vehicle is roadworthy and that it will not cause a hazard to other road users. Before leaving a quarry, check that the vehicle and its load will not compromise road safety. Make sure that mud or debris will not be spread on the road from the wheels or underbody, and that the tailgate has been securely shut.

When driving a tipper truck and about to exit a quarry, what should a driver ensure? C0086R
That the tailboard is secured.

When driving a HGV, you must make sure that the vehicle is roadworthy and that it will not cause a hazard to other road users. Before leaving a quarry, check tht the vehicle and its load will not compromise road safety. Make sure that mud or debris will not be spread on the road from the wheels or underbody, and that the tailgate has been securely shut. Also make sure that rear lights and reflectors are clean.

How does harsh acceleration affect fuel consumption?

ABMW0715

Fuel consumption increases.

Harsh acceleration increases fuel consumption, and driving smoothly helps to reduce your fuel consumption and the emissions from your vehicle. Try not to over-rev the engine and use the appropriate gear for the speed of the vehicle. When slowing down, take your foot off the accelerator and allow the vehicle to slow progressively before you brake.

What should a driver do to minimise fuel consumption in their vehicle?

Use gentle acceleration and braking.

ABMW0716R

Driving smoothly will help reduce your fuel consumption. Read the road ahead and adjust your speed in good time, and avoid harsh acceleration and late braking.

How does continuous high-speed driving affect fuel consumption?

It increases fuel consumption.

ABMW0717R

Driving at high speeds increases your fuel consumption. A vehicle travelling at 112km/h uses approximately 30% more fuel than one travelling at 80km/h.

What should a driver do to ensure better fuel efficiency from their vehicle?

ABMW0718R

Ensure that the vehicle is regularly serviced.

One of the keys to good fuel efficiency is making sure that your vehicle is well maintained. Servicing should be carried out as recommended by the manufacturer. Checking the tyre pressure regularly can also help ensure good fuel efficiency.

How can fuel efficiency be improved?

ABMW0719R

By using gentle acceleration and making gear changes appropriate to speed.

The way you drive can contribute to your vehicle's fuel efficiency: * Accelerate gently; * Use the highest available gear (without causing the engine to struggle); and * Drive smoothly – this also reduces wear and tear on a vehicle.

What effect does a worn exhaust have on a vehicle?

ABMW0720R

It causes noise and gas pollution levels to increase.

A vehicle with a worn exhaust will probably be noisier and will produce more polluting emissions. There are strict regulations governing the noise and emission levels of vehicles, and these are rigorously checked during a vehicle's NCT.

In what way do motor vehicles harm the environment?
ABMW0725R

By increasing carbon monoxide levels.

Carbon monoxide is a poisonous gas emitted by vehicle exhausts into the atmosphere. Driving economically and keeping a vehicle well maintained can reduce the level of carbon monoxide emissions.

What can a driver do to maximise fuel efficiency while driving?
ABMW0727R

Avoid carrying unnecessary weight.

The more extra weight is in your vehicle, the more fuel you use. Using a roof rack or a roof box increases wind resistance and this also increases fuel consumption – by as much as 15%. Remove roof racks and roof boxes when not in use.

Which action is likely to cause an increase in fuel consumption?
ABMW0728R

Harsh acceleration.

Harsh acceleration increases fuel consumption. Driving smoothly reduces wear and tear and also improves fuel consumption. Use the highest gear possible without causing the engine to labour.

What alternatives can drivers take to help protect the environment?

Use public transport.
ABMW0729R

Using public transport helps to protect the environment. Buses, trams and trains are a more environmentally friendly way to move large numbers of people especially in urban areas. Consider using public transport where possible – not only is it more environmentally friendly, but it can also be more cost-effective when you take the cost of fuel and parking charges into account.

What can be achieved by the driving style known as 'Eco-Driving'?

Reduced fuel consumption.
ABMW0730R

The advantages of 'eco-driving' include improved road safety, improved fuel consumption and reduced emissions. The eco-conscious driver becomes a more efficient driver because they learn to read the road further ahead and display better anticipation skills. This reduces the need for harsh acceleration and braking which results in a more economical style of driving and a smoother drive.

Which action contributes to Eco-Driving?
ABMW0731R

Selecting a high gear as soon as possible.

Eco-driving' contributes to road safety and also reduces fuel consumption and harmful emissions. Eco-conscious drivers will read the road well in advance and avoid harsh acceleration and braking. Fuel consumption can be reduced by using the highest gear possible without causing the engine to labour.

Vehicle Checks

When carrying out a Walk-around Check of the vehicle, the driver should ensure that tyres CD1306
are correctly inflated.

The daily Walk-around Check is an essential first step in an effective preventative maintenance system. Part of the check is to ensure that tyres are correctly inflated.

When carrying out an In Cab Check of the vehicle, the driver should ensure that CD1308
the horn is working properly.

The daily Walk-around Check is an essential first step in an effective preventative maintenance system. Part of the in-cab portion of the check is to ensure that the horn is working correctly.

When carrying out a Walk-around Check of the vehicle, the driver should ensure that mirrors CD1309
are correctly aligned.

The daily Walk-around Check is an essential first step in an effective preventative maintenance system. Part of the check is to ensure that mirrors are correctly aligned.

When carrying out a Walk-around Check of the vehicle, the driver should ensure that the exhaust is CD1310
has no excessive smoke.

The daily Walk-around Check is an essential first step in an effective preventative maintenance system. Part of the check is to ensure that mirrors are correctly aligned.

When carrying out a Walk-around Check of the vehicle, the driver should check the fuel cap for CD1311
leaks.

The daily Walk-around Check is an essential first step in an effective preventative maintenance system. Part of the check is to ensure that the fuel cap is in good condition and has no leaks.

When carrying out an In Cab Check of the vehicle, the driver should ensure which of the following is working properly? CD1312
Demister.

The daily Walk-around Check is an essential first step in an effective preventative maintenance system. Part of the in-cab portion of the check is to ensure that the demister is working correctly.

When carrying out a Walk-around Check of the vehicle, the driver should ensure that the lights CD1313
are clean.

The daily Walk-around Check is an essential first step in an effective preventative maintenance system. Part of the check is to ensure that the lights are clean.

With regard to vehicle checks, which of the following should the driver check after the Walk-around Check and prior to leaving the depot? CD1314
Steering is operating correctly.

After the Walk-around check there are some further checks the driver should make with the engine started, before leaving the depot / station. One of these checks is to ensure that the steering is operating correctly.

With regard to vehicle checks, which of the following should the driver check when on-the-road? CD1315
Speed limiter is operating correctly.

Once on the road, there are some ongoing checks the driver should make in the first few kilometres. One of these checks is to ensure the speed limiter is working correctly.

With regard to vehicle checks, which of the following should the driver check when on-the-road? CD1316
ABS/EBS warning lights are off.

Once on the road, there are some ongoing checks the driver should make in the first few kilometres. One of these checks is to ensure that the ABS or EBS lights do not remain on after their check sequence is complete, as this may indicate a fault in the system.

With regard to vehicle checks, which of the following should the driver check when on-the-road?

CD1317

Speedometer is operating correctly.

Once on the road, there are some ongoing checks the driver should make in the first few kilometres. One of these checks is to ensure the speedometer is working correctly.

What should the driver check before leaving the cab of a bus?

D8A

That it is safe to disembark the bus.

When parking a bus, you should make sure that it is in a safe place, the parking brake is on, the engine is switched off, and the electrical master switch is off. Before leaving the cab, check for approaching traffic to make sure it is safe to disembark.

Which of the following must a driver do when carrying out a walkaround check?

RSA01032

All mirrors are correctly aligned.

It is a legal requirement to have mirrors aligned on a bus before it leaves the garage.

Which of the following is an essential internal PSV check required prior to driving a bus?

RSA01035

Fire extinguisher, first aid kit, emergency hammer are in place and serviceable.

Under Health and safety these items are required in case of an emergency.

Which of the following is an essential PSV check required prior to driving a bus?

RSA01036

Emergency exit door operates freely and buzzer sounds at all times.

Under Health and safety the emergency door must be clearly marked and accessible at all time. It must never have locks on it or be locked/restricted at any time as it is required in case of an emergency.

TECHNICAL MATTERS » VEHICLE CHECKS

Which of the following is an essential interior PSV walk around check required on a bus? RSA01037

Passenger safety belts, seats, handrails, walkways, lighting and luggage racks are in good condition.

Passenger safety belts must operate no cuts or fraying. Seats fixed in place, not broken in anyway. Handrails no sharp edges and fixed in place. Walkways are clear and carpets fixed in place, no uneven surfaces liable to cause tripping. Lighting working to give clear walkways. Luggage racks fixed in place with restraints secure.

Which of the following must a driver do when carrying out a Bus In Cab check? RSA01038

Good visibility for driver through bus windows and mirrors.

The bus driver must have all round visibility.

Which of the following is an External Vehicle Check that must be carried out by the driver? RSA01039

The vehicle access, steps, handholds and surfaces are in good condition.

Access must be clear to avoid falls. All fixed restraints like hand rails are secure with no movement. No raised or sharp protrusions on all types of surfaces.

Which of the following should be checked on a bus prior to Leaving Depot? RSA01040

Luggage door is secure.

Before leaving the depot drivers must check that Steering and Brakes operate correctly and that luggage doors are secure.

1
2

Which of the following needs to be confirmed before the bus leaves the depot? RSA01041
ABS/EBS warning lights are working.

All warning lights must operate on a bus before it leaves the depot/garage.

Which of the following is included in the Bus In Cab Check? RSA01042
Driving controls, seat and driver safety belt adjusted correctly.

All controls must be working correctly to drive the bus safely and the driver must be secure in his seat and be able to control the bus safely from his seat.

Which of the following must a driver do when carrying out a Bus In Cab check? RSA01043
Ensure the windscreen washer, wipers, demister and horn are operating correctly.

In Cab checks must ensure good visibility for drivers through bus windows and mirrors. Checking that all mirrors are fitted and adjusted correctly and windscreen washer, wipers demister and horn all operate correctly.

What items should a driver check when carrying out an external walkaround? RSA01044
Wheel nut pointers are aligned where fitted.

Wheel nut pointers will give early warning on wheel nuts coming loose. It is also essential you visually check that the nuts are not loose.

Braking Systems

What is one major difference between air brakes and hydraulic vacuum servo brakes? CPC1024

One draws air from the atmosphere while the other draws vacuum from the engine.

Some smaller vehicles have hydraulic vacuum servo brakes which draw vacuum from the engine. This adds to the hydraulic pressure used to engage the brakes. Larger vehicles mainly use air brakes. These store air drawn from the atmosphere and then use it to engage the brakes. Air brakes do not use hydraulic fluid.

Where is the air that is used in the air brake systems stored? CPC1028

Reservoir tanks.

Air braking systems work closely with a compressor and draw air from the atmosphere to store them in reservoir tanks.

How do endurance braking systems (EBS) control vehicle speed? CPC1029

Without using the wheel-mounted brakes.

EBS improves vehicle control, reaction and vehicle stability during braking by using electronic signals to operate pneumatic valves. These apply resistance through the gearbox to help reduce the speed of the vehicle.

How does the driver know that a vehicle's anti-lock braking system (ABS) is engaged? CPC1032

A warning light will come on.

You can check that the ABS is working from a warning signal on the dashboard. How the warning lamp works may vary between manufacturers, but with all types the light comes on with the ignition.

What system helps to reduce brake failure due to high temperatures?
Endurance braking system. CPC1036

Endurance braking systems (EBS) help to control vehicle speed without using wheel-mounted brakes which operate on the principle of friction. The EBS apply resistance via the transmission to the rotation of the vehicle's driven wheels.

Which method uses exhaust braking to slow a vehicle's wheels?
Retarders. CPC1037

Retarders can be mechanical, electrical or hydraulic. Mechanical retarders can alter the engine exhaust flow to slow the vehicle without using wheel-mounted brakes. This is called exhaust braking.

What must the driver do before engaging the forward drive on a vehicle with an automatic gearbox? CPC1039
Hold the footbrake firmly.

Most vehicles have an interlock system which will not allow you to engage the automatic transmission unless the brake pedal is down. If you don't hold the brake while shifting into 'drive', the vehicle will lurch forward and may create a dangerous situation.

In what situation are endurance braking systems especially useful?
Coming down long hills. CPC1046

Endurance braking systems (EBS) are especially useful when descending long hills. You can reduce the vehicle's speed without using the service brake. This helps prevent the brakes from overheating (brake fade).

When travelling down a hill, the driver should CPC1048
first use the service brake to slow the vehicle.

The service brake is the main braking system to use when coming down a hill because it controls the vehicle speed.

If the driver constantly applies the brakes on a long downhill stretch it can result in
CPC1049A

brake fade.

When you brake for a long period, it generates heat and that heat contributes to brake fade. This means the drum heats up and expands away from the brake linings so that they are less effective.

Coming down a long hill, how can the driver avoid poor brake performance due to high heat?
CPC1050

Use the endurance brake.

If you use the service brake too much it generates heat, and braking performance can be reduced at high temperatures. Using the endurance braking systems properly reduces the use of the service brake.

What can cause ice to form in the valves and pipes of air brake systems?
Moisture in the air.
CPC1053

Air braking systems draw air from the atmosphere, which contains moisture. The moisture condenses in the air reservoirs and can travel around the braking system. In cold weather this can lead to ice forming in valves and pipes.

What happens when air pressure drops below normal in one of the brake reservoirs?
CPC1054

A warning light comes on.

Air brake systems are fitted with warning devices that activate when air pressure drops below normal level. This is usually a light and a warning sound.

The driver can check that brake warning devices are working by
turning on the ignition
CPC1055

You can and should check ABS warning lights before every journey. ABS warning signals will operate as soon as you turn the ignition on.

1
2

Road speed limiters work by
reducing fuel to the engine.

CPC1397

Road speed limiters receive a road speed signal from a sensor or the tachograph. They use that signal to reduce the amount of fuel to the engine.

How can a driver reduce speed without using the footbrake?
By lifting their foot off the accelerator.

CD9

If a driver reads the road ahead and reacts early enough, they can generally (unless going downhill) reduce speed simply by taking their foot off the accelerator. This style of driving prolongs the life of the vehicle's brakes, reduces fuel consumption and emissions, and improves passenger comfort.

What does a speed limiter do?
Prevents the vehicle from exceeding a pre-set speed.

CD0058R

A speed limiter is a device fitted to HGVs and buses which sets the maximum speed at which the vehicle can travel.

How does an engine governor control an engine?
Prevents the engine from over revving.

CD0059A

An engine governor is a device fitted to the engine's fuel pump. It limits or controls the amount of fuel delivered to the engine, and prevents the engine from over-revving.

Given similar road conditions and vehicle speeds, what braking distances will a truck or bus/minibus need compared to a car?
Longer distances.

CD0061R

When driving a car on a good road in good weather, the driver should leave at least a 2-second gap between them and the vehicle in front. A larger vehicle needs a bigger gap, because of its greater weight and momentum. The driver should allow at least a 4-second gap under normal conditions, and even more on wet or icy roads.

How can a driver reduce speed without using the footbrake? CD0060R
By engaging the retarder, if fitted.

Endurance braking systems (or retarders) are standard equipment on many trucks and buses. They enable the driver to reduce speed without using the wheel-mounted brake (or service brake). Retarders are particularly useful when descending hills, as they help to extend the life of the brakes and to prevent brake fade.

On a vehicle equipped with an air-brake system, what is the first indication of low air-pressure? CD0062R
A warning light comes on and /or a buzzer sounds in the cab.

Most modern HGVs and buses are fitted with air brakes. If air pressure drops in the braking system, a warning light and/or buzzer alerts the driver. The driver should pull in and stop safely before total loss of air pressure.

After moderate use of the brakes, a driver notices that the air-gauges are not returning to normal. What should the driver do? CD0063R
Stop safely and build up air pressure.

Most modern HGVs and buses are fitted with air brakes. If, after moderate use of the brakes, the air pressure gauges do not return to normal, the driver should stop in a safe place and try to build up air pressure. If the gauges remain low, the driver should suspect an air leak, and not drive the vehicle until it is rectified. Driving with an air leak can cause the brakes to lock on and immobilise the vehicle, which could cause an obstruction or a hazard to other traffic.

What does a warning buzzer in the cab indicate usually? C0028R
Low air pressure in the braking system.

Vehicles fitted with air brakes are equipped with a buzzer to alert the driver to a loss of air pressure. You should not attempt to drive while this buzzer is sounding. If the buzzer comes on when you are driving, pull over in a safe place as soon as possible. If your vehicle loses all air pressure, the brakes may lock on, which may cause an obstruction or hazard to other traffic.

Driving Large or High-Sided Vehicles

Driving in Strong Winds / an Unfamiliar Vehicle

What effect can strong winds have on a high-sided vehicle?
They can increase the likelihood of the vehicle overturning. CD0106R

When driving a high-sided vehicle in strong winds, the driver should choose a route that avoids high-level roads and bridges, exposed motorways and dual carriageways.

When driving a high-sided vehicle in strong winds, what should a driver avoid? CD0107R
Suspension bridges.

When driving a high-sided vehicle in strong winds, the driver should choose a route that avoids high-level roads and bridges, exposed motorways and dual carriageways.

What would help to stabilise a high-sided vehicle in windy conditions?
Having a full load. CD0108R

A high-sided vehicle being driven in strong winds is more stable if it has a full, evenly distributed load.

Why is a large vehicle likely to intimidate other road users?
The size and noise of the vehicle. CD0109R

Other road users can be intimidated by the sheer size and noise of a large vehicle, but the driver should never deliberately frighten other road users, for example by revving the engine, by driving too close to them or by repeatedly pressing the footbrake to create loud hissing noises.

When someone is driving a vehicle that is different to the vehicle they normally drive or with which they are unfamiliar, what should they do?
Drive initially with extra care and at a lower speed than normal.   CD0110R

If you are required to drive a vehicle that is different to the vehicle you normally drive or with which you are unfamiliar, you should take time to familiarise yourself with the controls and operating systems. When driving the vehicle initially you should take extra care and drive at lower speeds than usual until you become accustomed to the vehicle.

When someone is driving a vehicle that has features with which the driver is unfamiliar, what in particular should the driver be aware of?
The height, weight, length and width and/or the controls may differ from the vehicle usually driven by the driver.   CD0112R

If you are required to drive a vehicle with which you are unfamiliar, you should take time to familiarise yourself with the controls and operating systems. You should also learn the height, length, width and weight of the vehicle, so that you can comply with any restrictions you meet on the road.

What effect can strong winds have on a high-sided vehicle?
The winds can reduce the vehicle's stability.   CD0113R

When driving a high-sided vehicle in strong winds, the driver should choose a route that avoids high-level roads and bridges, exposed motorways and dual carriageways.

A truck or bus that is not equipped with anti-lock brakes (ABS) goes into a front-wheel skid. What should the driver do?   CD0165R
Pump the footbrake.

If you are driving a truck or bus that is not equipped with ABS and a front-wheel skid develops, pump the footbrake rapidly. This is known as 'cadence braking' and it can prevent or stop a vehicle from skidding.

General 1

When driving a large vehicle, why is it sometimes necessary to move to the right before making a left-hand turn? CD0116R

To ensure the nearside rear wheels clear the corner.

If you are driving a long vehicle and wish to turn left into a narrow road, take as much room as you need on the approach to the junction to allow you to complete the turn without your nearside rear wheels mounting the footpath. This may mean that your vehicle will be to the right of its normal position on the road, and other road users, especially cyclists, may come up on the inside of your vehicle.

A driver is driving a long vehicle and wishes to turn left into a narrow side road. What should the driver do? CD0114R

Be aware that cyclists may come up on the inside if the vehicle has moved to the right to make room to turn left.

If you are driving a long vehicle and wish to turn left into a narrow road, take as much room as you need on the approach to the junction to allow you to complete the turn successfully. This may mean that your vehicle will be to the right of its normal position on the road, and other road users, especially cyclists, may come up on the inside of your vehicle.

A driver is driving a long vehicle and wishes to turn left into a narrow side road. What should a driver do? CD0115R

Move to the right on the approach to allow the turn be made without mounting the kerb.

If you are driving a long vehicle and wish to turn left into a narrow road, take as much room as you need on the approach to the junction to allow you to complete the turn successfully. This may mean that your vehicle will be to the right of its normal position on the road, and other road users, especially cyclists, may come up on the inside of your vehicle.

When driving a large vehicle on a road which has overhanging trees, what should a driver do? CD0120R

Drive in the normal position but move out as necessary to avoid hitting overhanging branches.

When driving a large vehicle on a road that has overhanging trees, maintain your normal position on the road as far as possible, but move out as necessary to avoid hitting the trees, and return to the normal position as soon as you can.

1
2

When driving a low-loader vehicle, what should a driver allow for?
Narrow bridges.   CD0121R

A low loader is a semi-trailer used to transport heavy oversized vehicles. When loaded, it may be higher, wider and lower than a standard vehicle. If you are driving such a vehicle, you should be aware of these extra hazards and plan your route accordingly, avoiding, where necessary, obstacles such as humpback or narrow bridges and overhead cables.

When driving an articulated car-transporter, what should a driver be aware of?
CD0122R

The front overhang follows a wider line than the cab.

The driver of a car transporter should be aware of the extra height of the vehicle when it is loaded with the cars, the instability of the vehicle when only the top deck is loaded, and, on articulated car transporters, the fact that front overhang does not follow the line of the cab when turning.

When driving an articulated car-transporter, what should a driver be aware of?
CD0123R

The front overhang follows a wider line than the cab.

The driver of a car transporter should be aware of the extra height of the vehicle when it is loaded with the cars, the instability of the vehicle when only the top deck is loaded, and, on articulated car transporters, the fact that front overhang does not follow the line of the cab when turning.

When driving a car-transporter, what should a driver plan ahead for?
Low bridges.   CD0124RA

The driver of a car transporter should be aware of the extra height of the vehicle when it is loaded with the cars, the instability of the vehicle when only the top deck is loaded, and, on articulated car transporters, the fact that front overhang does not follow the line of the cab when turning.

How should following traffic be warned in the event of an incident?
By placing a red warning triangle on the road a short distance back from the vehicle involved.   CD0166R

If your vehicle breaks down, or is involved in an incident, place a red warning triangle on the road, far enough from the incident to give following traffic adequate warning.

Under what circumstances should a driver use an emergency red warning triangle?
CD0167R

In the event of an incident or breakdown.

If your vehicle breaks down, or is involved in an incident, place a red warning triangle on the road, far enough from the incident to give following traffic adequate warning.

When driving a car transporter, what should a driver plan ahead for?
CD17

Overhanging trees.

The driver of a car transporter should be aware of the extra height of the vehicle when it is loaded with the cars, the instability of the vehicle when only the top deck is loaded, and, on articulated car transporters, the fact that front overhang does not follow the line of the cab when turning.

When driving a car transporter, what should a driver plan ahead for?
CD18

Overhead cables.

The driver of a car transporter should be aware of the extra height of the vehicle when it is loaded with the cars, the instability of the vehicle when only the top deck is loaded, and, on articulated car transporters, the fact that front overhang does not follow the line of the cab when turning.

What effect does increasing the load have on the vehicle's braking ability?
C0041A

It increases the normal stopping distance required.

In general, a heavier load makes a truck more difficult to stop and increases the required stopping distance.

What should a driver do before moving off from a stop where the wheelchair ramp was used by a passenger?
RSA01015

Ensure that the wheelchair ramp is safely secured.

Before moving away from a stop where the wheelchair ramp was used, you should always ensure the ramp safely secured in its location for safety reasons.

Who is responsible for ensuring a valid Road Passenger Operators Licence Disc is affixed to the vehicle?
RSA01016

Vehicle Driver.

It is responsibility of a driver and operator, to put proper arrangements in place to make sure that, where relevant, each vehicle complies with the requirements to display the Road Passenger Operators Licence Disc.

Why is AdBlue or Diesel Exhaust Fluid added to the fuel system?

It reduces the oxides of ammonia in diesel fuel emissions.
RSA01033

AdBlue is a non-toxic liquid that's colourless in appearance and is a solution of water and urea. To comply with Euro 5 and Euro 6 diesel-powered trucks, buses and cars use Selective Catalytic Reduction technology to inject microscopic quantities of this liquid into the flow of exhaust gases. When the urea and water solution combines with exhaust emissions, it produces nitrogen and oxygen. Harmless gases that occur naturally in the environment, by breaking down mono-nitrogen oxides (gases that can be harmful and are found particularly in the fumes from diesel exhausts).

Why should you monitor the levels of AdBlue or Diesel Exhaust Fluid?

It reduces the oxides of ammonia in diesel fuel emissions.
RSA01034

AdBlue is a non-toxic liquid that's colourless in appearance and is a solution of water and urea. To comply with Euro 5 and Euro 6 diesel-powered trucks, buses and cars use Selective Catalytic Reduction technology to inject microscopic quantities of this liquid into the flow of exhaust gases. When the urea and water solution combines with exhaust emissions, it produces nitrogen and oxygen. Harmless gases that occur naturally in the environment, by breaking down mono-nitrogen oxides (gases that can be harmful and are found particularly in the fumes from diesel exhausts).

General 2

What should a driver of a tipper truck be aware of when tipping a load from their vehicle?
C0047RA

Underground cable and power lines. Overhead cables and power lines.

Before raising the tipper body, check to see that there are no overhead cables or power lines that could be touched by the raised body. Failure to make this check could prove fatal.

Knowing the height of the vehicle is important in order to avoid an accident involving
CPC1148

bridges.

Many bridges are hit by vehicles which are too high to pass underneath. You should know your vehicle height and pay attention to restriction signs.

When driving a large vehicle around a roundabout, what precaution should the driver take to avoid roll-over?
CD0126R

Reduce speed.

A vehicle can become unstable and roll over if it changes direction sharply while being driven too fast. For this reason, when driving a large vehicle, you should slow down on approaching a roundabout to reduce the likelihood of rolling over.

What in particular should a driver be aware of when driving a low-bodied vehicle over a steep humpback bridge?
CD0128R

Ground clearance.

When driving a vehicle with a low body, you should take care that the vehicle is not 'grounded'. You need to make sure that you have sufficient ground clearance when, for example, going over railway level crossings or humpback bridges.

What should a driver be aware of when driving a vehicle that has a high centre of gravity? CD0131R

The vehicle is more likely to roll over on a bend or roundabout.

If you are driving a large vehicle with a high centre of gravity, you should slow down on bends, corners and roundabouts. The vehicle can become unstable and roll over if it changes direction sharply while being driven too fast.

A driver is driving a large vehicle up a steep hill. There is a 'slow lane' on the left. What should the driver do? CD0133R

Drive in the slow lane.

Slow lanes (also known as crawler or climbing lanes) have been introduced on some roads to allow large slow-moving vehicles get out of the way of faster-moving traffic. When driving a large vehicle, you should use such lanes where possible to help improve traffic flow.

1

2

The driver of a large vehicle needs to proceed straight ahead at a mini roundabout at which there is limited space to manoeuvre. What should the driver do? CD0134R

To the extent possible, negotiate the mini roundabout in the same way as a normal roundabout.

Mini-roundabouts generally function as traffic calming measures. They do not always provide sufficient room for a large vehicle to negotiate them in the same way as a normal roundabout. The driver must evaluate the situation on approach and respond in a way that is appropriate for the size of their vehicle, while yielding as appropriate to other traffic.

Overtaking

What should the driver of a large vehicle consider before overtaking another large vehicle?
CD0136R

The speed of the vehicle being overtaken.

Before overtaking another large vehicle, the driver of a large vehicle needs to assess the road ahead, and take into consideration the speed of the vehicle they are driving and the speed of the vehicle they intend overtaking. They should be sure that they can complete the manoeuvre safely. Overtaking a large vehicle with a large vehicle takes more time and greater distance than a similar manoeuvre involving two cars.

What should the driver of a large vehicle consider before overtaking another large vehicle?
CD0137R

The width and condition of the road.

Before overtaking another large vehicle, the driver of a large vehicle needs to assess the road ahead, and take into consideration the size and speed of the vehicle they are driving and the size and speed of the vehicle they intend overtaking. They should be sure that they can complete the manoeuvre safely. Extra clearance is needed to overtake wider vehicles safely. If the road is uneven, the stability of the vehicle can be affected. The driver may need to wait for a safer place to overtake.

After overtaking another large vehicle, what should a driver do before moving back into the left-hand lane?
CD0138R

Check the left-hand mirror, signal, and move back when it is safe to do so.

Before overtaking a large vehicle on a dual carriageway or motorway, you should check your right-hand mirror, signal and move out into the right-hand lane when it is safe to do so. After overtaking the vehicle, check your left-hand mirror, signal and move back in to the left-hand lane when it is safe to do so. Do not cut too quickly across the vehicle you have just passed.

In which of the following situations is overtaking on the left permitted?
The driver has signalled that they intend to turn left.
CD1326

Drivers must normally overtake on the right. However, overtaking on the left is allowed in some situations, including when the driver has signalled that they intend to turn left.

When going straight ahead at a roundabout, a driver should give way to
Traffic coming from the right.
CD1327

At the majority of roundabouts, for safety and to maintain the flow of traffic, approaching traffic is required to give way to traffic coming from the right.

Vehicle Weights and Dimensions

Trucks and buses can vary considerably in length, height and weight.

When you are driving a bus or a truck, you need to develop an understanding and awareness of where you are on the road in relation to other vehicles, to street furniture (such as bollards and lamp posts) and to other objects – including road signs, overhanging trees, traffic islands and so on. Coming to terms with the size of the particular vehicle you are driving is essential.

You also need to know details about the weight of your vehicle, and the weight bearing on each axle. EU and national rules govern the maximum weights of different kinds of truck and bus, and you are responsible for ensuring that your vehicle is in compliance.

What is the maximum permitted rear load overhang that does not require a red flag or marker?   CD0042A
1 metre.

In order to warn other road users, loads extending from the rear of a vehicle by more than 1 metre must be clearly marked with a red flag or marker by day and by a lamp by night. The overhang must not exceed 3 metres.

What is the maximum permitted rear load overhang with a red flag?
3 metres.   CD0043

In order to warn other road users, loads extending from the rear of a vehicle by more than 1 metre must be clearly marked with a red flag or marker by day and by a lamp by night. The overhang must not exceed 3 metres.

When is a red flag a sufficient marker for a rear-load overhang that exceeds one metre?   CD0045
Only during the day.

In order to warn other road users, loads extending from the rear of a vehicle by more than 1 metre must be clearly marked with a red flag or marker by day and by a lamp by night. The overhang must not exceed 3 metres.

What is the maximum permitted side-load overhang in millimetres?
305mm.

CD0046R

The maximum side-load overhang normally permitted is 305 millimetres (1 foot). To carry a load with a greater overhang, you need an abnormal load permit, which can be obtained from An Garda Síochána.

What is the maximum permitted length of an articulated vehicle?
16.5 metres.

CD0047R

The maximum permitted length of an articulated vehicle is 16.5 metres. To drive a longer vehicle or load, you must apply for permits from the Local Authorities of the areas through which you will be driving and/or An Garda Síochána.

What is the Maximum Authorised Mass (M.A.M) of an articulated truck with six axles?
46 Tonnes.

C0016A

1

2

An articulated truck with a GVW of 44 tonnes is required to have six axles, anti-lock brakes and air suspension.

What is the Maximum Authorised Mass (M.A.M) in tonnes of a 4-axle rigid truck with conventional (non air) suspension?
30 Tonnes.

C0018AA

The maximum permitted laden weight of a 4-axle rigid truck with conventional suspension is 30 tonnes. Overloading any truck is illegal and can have serious consequences.

What is the Maximum Authorised Mass (M.A.M) in tonnes of a 4-axle rigid truck with road friendly (air) suspension?
32 Tonnes.

C0019A

The maximum permitted laden weight of a 4-axle rigid truck with road-friendly suspension is 32 tonnes. Overloading any truck is illegal and can have serious consequences.

What is the Maximum Authorised Mass (M.A.M) in tonnes of a 3-axle rigid truck with conventional (non air) suspension?
25 Tonnes.

C0020A

The maximum permitted laden weight of a 3-axle rigid truck with conventional suspension is 25 tonnes. Overloading any truck is illegal and can have serious consequences.

is the Maximum Authorised Mass (M.A.M) in tonnes of a 2-axle rigid truck with conventional suspension? C0021AA
18 Tonnes.

The maximum permitted laden weight of a 2-axle rigid truck with conventional suspension is 18 tonnes. Overloading any truck is illegal and can have serious consequences.

What is the maximum width of a bus? D0017R
2.55 metres.

You should always know the width of your vehicle, and bear it in mind when driving beside parked vehicles or on narrow roads. The maximum permitted width of a bus is 2.55 metres.

What is the maximum height of a double-decker bus? D0018R
4.57 metres.

You should always know the height of your vehicle, and bear it in mind when driving in areas with restricted heights, such as low and arch bridges, and bus garage doors. A collision could result in serious or fatal injury to passengers. The maximum permitted height is 4.57 metres.

What is the maximum permitted length of a two-axle bus? D1300
13.5 metres.

Drivers should always know the length of their vehicle, and bear it in mind when required to judge safe distances, for example for overtaking. The maximum permitted length of a two-axle bus is 13.5 metres.

What is the maximum permitted length of a bus having more than two axles? D1301
15 metres.

Drivers should always know the length of their vehicle, and bear it in mind when required to judge safe distances, for example for overtaking. The maximum permitted length of a bus which has more than two axles is 15 metres.

What is the maximum permitted length of an articulated bus? D1302
18.75 metres.

Drivers should always know the length of their vehicle, and bear it in mind when required to judge safe distances, for example for overtaking. The maximum permitted length of a bus which has more than two axles is 18.75 metres.

What is the Maximum Authorised Mass (MAM) of a two-axle bus? D1303
18 Tonnes.

The maximum authorised mass of a two-axle bus is 18 tonnes. Overloading any vehicle is illegal and can have serious consequences.

What is the Maximum Authorised Mass (MAM) of a three-axle articulated bus? D1304
28 tonnes.

The maximum authorised mass of a three-axle articulated bus is 28 tonnes. Overloading any vehicle is illegal and can have serious consequences.

1

2

A bus is deemed to be carrying a full load of passengers if weights of how many kilograms are placed in the correct positions for the driver and each passenger? D1305
65 kg.

A driver should be aware of the weight of their vehicle. Overloading any vehicle is illegal and can have serious consequences.

Air Turbulence

Which type of road user is particularly badly affected by the air-turbulence caused by a passing high-sided vehicle? CD0093R
Pedestrians.

A high-sided vehicle creates air turbulence to the sides and rear of the vehicle, and this turbulence increases with the speed of the vehicle. This affects other road users, and in particular pedestrians, cyclists, motorcyclists and cars towing caravans. The driver should take extra care when passing such road users, to avoid blowing them off course.

What is the effect of a large vehicle's slipstream on a motorcyclist it is overtaking? CD0094R
The motorcyclist can be blown off course.

A high-sided vehicle creates air turbulence to the sides and rear of the vehicle, and this turbulence increases with the speed of the vehicle. The driver should take extra care when passing motorcyclists, to avoid blowing them off course.

What is the effect of a large vehicle's slipstream on a cyclist it is overtaking? CD0095R
It can affect the cyclist's stability.

A high-sided vehicle creates air turbulence to the sides and rear of the vehicle, and this turbulence increases with the speed of the vehicle. The driver should take extra care when passing cyclists to avoid affecting their stability.

What can happen if a vehicle displaces dust or debris from the road?
The dust and debris can discomfort pedestrians and make it difficult for them to see where they are going. CD0096R

Dust and debris displaced from the road by a large vehicle can make it difficult for other road users to see. This is both uncomfortable and unsafe.

What in particular should the driver of a large vehicle be aware of when passing pedestrians? CD0097R
The pedestrians can be affected by the vehicle's slipstream.

The driver of a large vehicle should always show due care and consideration for vulnerable road users such as pedestrians. This is particularly important in rural areas where there are no footpaths, and in bad weather. Spray, dust or debris thrown up from the wheels can make it difficult for the pedestrian to see, and the air turbulence created by the vehicle can blow them
off course.

What should the driver of a large vehicle be aware of when being overtaken by a motorcyclist in windy weather?
CD0135R

The wind turbulence will make the motorcycle less stable.

When a motorcyclist is overtaking a high-sided vehicle, the turbulence created by the larger vehicle may affect the motorcyclist's stability.

Which type of road user is particularly badly affected by the air-turbulence caused by a passing high-sided vehicle?
CD10

Cars towing caravans.

A high-sided vehicle creates air turbulence to the sides and rear of the vehicle, and this turbulence increases with the speed of the vehicle. This affects other road users, and in particular pedestrians, cyclists, motorcyclists and cars towing caravans. The driver should take extra care when passing such road users, to avoid blowing them off course.

Which type of road user is particularly badly affected by the air-turbulence caused by a passing high-sided vehicle?
CD11

Cyclists.

A high-sided vehicle creates air turbulence to the sides and rear of the vehicle, and this turbulence increases with the speed of the vehicle. This affects other road users, and in particular pedestrians, cyclists, motorcyclists and cars towing caravans. The driver should take extra care when passing such road users, to avoid blowing them off course.

Which type of road user is particularly badly affected by the air-turbulence caused by a passing high-sided vehicle?
CD12

Motorcyclists.

A high-sided vehicle creates air turbulence to the sides and rear of the vehicle, and this turbulence increases with the speed of the vehicle. This affects other road users, and in particular pedestrians, cyclists, motorcyclists and cars towing caravans. The driver should take extra care when passing such road users, to avoid blowing them off course.

1

2

Safety of Vehicle Loading

General

When stopping for a short period of time in an urban area, for example to let off passengers or unload goods, what should a driver do? CD0145R
Avoid causing an obstruction to other road users by parking close to the left.

When stopping or parking to deliver goods or collect passengers, you should stop in a location that does not cause obstruction to other road users.

How can overloading affect a vehicle? CD0146R
The vehicle's stability can be affected.

The effects of overloading a goods vehicle include damage to the road surfaces, damage to the vehicle itself, and loss of stability in the vehicle, possibly leading to a serious incident. Overloading is against the law, punishable by fines and imprisonment.

With regard to the load they are carrying what should a driver ensure?
That it does not cause danger or nuisance to other road users. C0037AA

You must make sure that your load is safely and securely loaded, and that the load is evenly distributed over the axles. Make sure also that the load does not pose any danger or inconvenience to other road users.

How might an unevenly distributed load affect a truck?
The truck's stability is adversely affected. C0039

You must make sure that your load is safely and securely loaded, and that the load is evenly distributed over the axles. An insecure or unbalanced load, or one that is too heavy, can compromise the safety and stability of the vehicle.

What effect does sharp braking have on a loosely secured load?
The load tends to go to the front of the vehicle. C0040

You must make sure that your load is safely and securely loaded. If you brake or change direction suddenly, an insecure load can shift or fall off, causing the vehicle to lose stability and creating a hazard for other road users.

1
2

What effect does increasing the load have on the vehicle's braking ability?
C0041

It increases the normal stopping distance required.

In general, a heavier load makes a truck more difficult to stop and increases the required stopping distance.

How does air suspension affect a vehicle's carrying capacity, compared to that of a vehicle with conventional suspension?
C0042R

It allows extra weight to be carried.

Air suspension (road-friendly suspension) provides the vehicle with an even load height, whether it is empty or fully laden. It allows for extra weight to be carried by the vehicle, and helps to protect fragile goods in transit.

What additional precautions should be taken when transporting bulk liquid?
C0043

The tanks should be sectioned off.

Where possible, vehicles that carry bulk liquids should have the tank divided up into sections or have baffle plates installed to reduce the wave effect and help the driver to slow or stop the vehicle smoothly.

How should a load of loose dusty material be carried?
C0044R

It should be covered with a tarpaulin or sheeting.

When dusty material, such as sand or grain, is carried, the load should be covered with a tarpaulin or sheeting to avoid the load being lost by blowing off the vehicle and creating a hazard or nuisance for other road users.

What should a driver ensure when carrying hazardous materials?
C0045R

That they comply with the regulations on the conveyance of dangerous substances by road.

If you are driving a vehicle that is carrying hazardous materials, you are responsible for taking all the appropriate precautions to ensure public safety. The driver must be qualified to transport the specific material and the vehicle must be equipped with the relevant safety equipment and labels.

What should a driver ensure when carrying out an inspection under a raised tipper body?
C0046R

That the body is supported by props.

Never carry out an inspection under a raised tipper body unless the body is properly supported by props. The prop used should be strong enough to hold the structure in place if the hydraulic raising system malfunctions.

What should a driver of a tipper truck be aware of when tipping a load from their vehicle?
C0047R

Overhead cables and power lines.

Before raising the tipper body, check to see that there are no overhead cables or power lines that could be touched by the raised body. Failure to make this check could prove fatal.

What effect may the liquid load have on an articulated tanker when it is braking to a stop on a straight road?
C0053R

It may push the vehicle forward.

When braking in an articulated tanker with a liquid load, you should be aware of the 'wave effect' caused by the motion of the fluid in the tank. This may cause the vehicle to surge forward when you ease pressure on the brakes.

What should a driver do when coming to a stop while driving a half loaded tanker which is not divided into compartments?
C0054R

Ease off the footbrake.

When braking in a partially loaded tanker, you should be aware of the 'wave effect' caused by the motion of the fluid in the tank. This may cause the vehicle to surge forward when you ease pressure on the brakes. For this reason you should ease off the brake gently.

Triangular projection markers must be used if the load overhangs the vehicle by
C1322

more than 2 metres.

Warning devices, such as triangular projection markers, help draw other road users' attention to an overhanging load, enabling them to maintain a safe distance from the vehicle and its load.

1
2

To secure loose bulk loads (e.g. sand) which of the following should be used? C1323
Sheeting cover.

Loose bulk loads, such as sand, are typically not packaged and are usually carried in open-bodied vehicles. As they are susceptible to displacement and blowing away, a suitable cover, such as sheeting, should be used to cover and protect the load.

A driver who transports dangerous goods must have which of the following? C1325
An ADR Driver Training Certificate.

A driver who transports dangerous goods must be certified on the specific technical requirements that have to be met during transport of dangerous goods. This certification is the ADR Driver Training Certificate.

When may the maximum weight which an axle is designed to carry be exceeded? C0050R
It may never be exceeded.

The maximum design weight of each axle and the maximum weight it is allowed to carry in Ireland (which may be less) must be displayed on a plate attached to the vehicle.

How is a lifting axle used? C0051R
It may be raised or lowered depending on the load being carried.

Rigid lorries, tractor units and trailers are often fitted with lifting axles. These axles may be free running or steered. The advantage of a lifting axle is that it can be raised or lowered to suit the load on the vehicle, thereby saving fuel and tyre wear.

Why are ropes unsuitable to tie down a load of girders? C0055R
Because they may wear and snap.

Sharp edges on the girders can cause the ropes to fray and snap, with the result that your load becomes insecure. If a load has sharp edges, you should use web straps with suitable sleeves to protect the webbing from the sharp edges.

Why should the cargo area of a truck carrying loose sand be covered?

C0056R

To prevent the sand from blowing away.

When dusty material, such as sand or grain, is carried, the load should be covered with a tarpaulin or sheeting to avoid the load being lost by blowing off the vehicle and creating a hazard or nuisance for other road users.

In what circumstances is an articulated truck more likely to jack-knife?

C0058R

When it is unloaded.

If, while driving an articulated truck, you brake sharply or slow down quickly, the trailer may pivot around the tow hitch coupling and cause both vehicles to go off course, and possibly overturn. This is more likely to occur on an unladen vehicle, where there is less weight on the driving axle.

Why is it important to distribute the weight evenly between the axles when loading a heavy goods vehicle?

C0059R

To ensure maximum stability.

To ensure the stability of your vehicle, you must make sure that the load is evenly distributed between the axles. In addition, the load should be secured against the headboard to prevent it from moving forward under braking, and heavy items should be placed at the bottom to prevent the vehicle from becoming top-heavy.

Loads should be arranged such that their centre of gravity is

C1321

as low as possible.

Ensuring that the load centre of gravity is as low as possible helps to ensure load security and stability. A load with a high centre of gravity is less secure and can compromise the safety and stability of the vehicle.

To securely load boxes, which of the following strategies should be used?

C1324

Tightly pack the boxes together.

Tightly packed boxes are less likely to move than those that are loosely packed, enhancing load security and safety.

An operator transporting a large load (25 metres in length) plans a journey which will take place entirely on designated roads. Which of the following permits does the operator require? C1326
Garda permit.

A Garda permit is required for a journey which takes place entirely on designated roads, by a vehicle and load which exceeds the regulation limits on the size of vehicles and loads, but which does not exceed 27.4 metres in length or 4.3 metres in width or 4.65 metres in height.

An operator transporting a large load (28 metres in length) plans a journey which will take place entirely on designated roads. Which of the following permits does the operator require? C1327
A Local Authority permit for each local authority area passed through.

A Local Authority permit is required for each Local Authority area passed through on a journey by a vehicle and load which exceeds 27.4 metres in length or 4.3 metres in width or 4.65 metres in height.

Who can be held responsible if a truck is found to be overloaded? C0061R
Both the driver and the owner.

Both the owner and the driver can be held responsible if a goods vehicle is found to be overloaded on a public road.

Who is responsible for making sure that a truck's load is secure during a journey? C0062RA
The driver.

It is the driver's responsibility to know how a vehicle has been loaded and how the load has been secured. You should also check your load at regular intervals, as it may settle or move during the journey, thereby causing the straps or chains to loosen.

What action should a driver take if they are required to make an urgent delivery of a container and notice that some of the twist locks or container securing devices are broken? C0064R
They should not drive until the twist-locks have been repaired or replaced.

The driver is responsible for the security of their load. If the twist locks are defective on a container-carrying vehicle, the container could fall off the vehicle on a bend or roundabout, causing damage to property and creating a hazard for other road users.

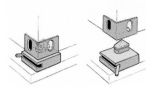

What are twist locks used to secure? C0065R

A steel cargo container onto a vehicle or trailer.

Twist locks are used to secure a steel container to a flat or skeletal trailer. The driver must make sure that the twist locks are in the unlocked position when the container is being lifted on or off the trailer, and that they are in the locked position when the vehicle in is transit.

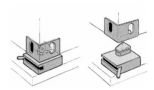

How should an ISO cargo container be secured to a vehicle? C0071R

With twist locks.

Lift on/Lift off ISO containers should be carried only on skeletal trailers or flat bed trailers equipped with proper twist locks. You must ensure that these twist locks are locked into the container while in transit.

1

2

How should steel girders be loaded on a vehicle? C0066R

In such a way that the weight is evenly distributed on the vehicle.

Steel girders should be loaded against the headboard of the vehicle, and their weight distributed evenly between the axles to ensure stability. They should be secured with strong chains or similar devices. If web straps are used, the webbing should be protected where it passes over the corners of the girders.

What should a driver ensure when their load consists of steel girders?

That the girders are properly secured with strong chains or similar devices. C0067R

Steel girders should be loaded against the headboard of the trailer and secured with strong chains or similar devices. If web straps are used, the webbing should be protected where it passes over the corners of the girders. Drivers should stop at regular intervals during the journey to check the tension of the chains or straps.

How should a load of steel scaffolding poles be secured? C0068RA
Secured firmly with strong chains or similar devices.

Steel scaffolding poles should be loaded against the headboard of the trailer and secured with strong chains or similar devices. The driver should stop at regular intervals during the journey to check the tension of the chains or straps.

What should a driver check before reversing into a loading bay? C0072RA
For the presence of other people.

When reversing in haulage and distribution yards, you must watch out for people getting in and out of adjacent vehicles and pedestrians who may walk behind the vehicle.

When driving a truck with hazardous goods or substances, who is responsible for ensuring that a Hazchem sign is displayed? C0078A
The driver.

If you are driving a truck carrying hazardous goods, you must ensure that the correct symbol or mark is clearly displayed on the vehicle. In the event of a collision, the information provided by the sign provides vital information for the emergency services.

What is the maximum permitted distance between a drawing vehicle and a trailer? C0081R
4.5 metres.

The maximum permitted distance between a drawing vehicle and a trailer is 4.5 metres. A larger distance between the vehicles might lead other road users to believe that the two vehicles were independent and they might try to enter the space between them.

A warning device or flag must be attached to a drawbar when it exceeds what length? C0082R
1.5 metres.

The maximum permitted distance between a drawing vehicle and a trailer is 4.5 metres. Where it exceeds 1.5 metres, a warning device, such as a white flag of at least 30 centimetres, must be attached, to draw attention to the tow bar.

Dealing with Forces Acting on the Vehicle

Resistance to change in a vehicle's motion is called
CPC1042A
inertia.

Resistance to movement is called inertia. The opposite of this is momentum – the force that keeps vehicles in motion.

The force that keeps a vehicle moving is called
CPC1043A
momentum.

The force that keeps a vehicle in motion (moving) is called momentum.

How does acceleration and braking affect people sitting in a vehicle?
Acceleration pushes passengers back while braking moves them
CPC1045AAA
forward.

Acceleration will push passengers back, while braking will push them forward. A person's inertia must be overcome in much the same way as the vehicle's inertia.

1
2

The amount of grip a tyre has on a road surface depends on which of the following factors?
CD1329
Vehicle weight.

Grip produces traction, which allows a vehicle to accelerate, change direction and slow down. Understanding the factors which affect grip is critical to safe and effective driving. One such factor is vehicle weight.

When a vehicle is stationary on level ground, the only force generally acting on it is
CD1330
gravity.

When not on an uphill or downhill gradient, and when not in motion, typically the only force acting on a vehicle is the downward pull of gravity.

The effect of cornering force on people sitting in a vehicle is to throw them
CD1331
towards the outside of the bend.

To ensure passenger comfort and safety, drivers should avoid taking bends too fast, as cornering force in this instance causes passengers to be thrown toward the outside of the bend.

The energy held by a moving vehicle is referred to as kinetic.

CD1332

When travelling, energy is stored up in a vehicle and its passengers. This energy is kinetic energy.

On a downhill gradient, which of the following effects will gravity have?
Increase stopping distances.

CD1333

On a downhill gradient, gravity makes the vehicle's speed increase, therefore stopping distances and the braking effort required to slow the vehicle are also increased.

On an uphill gradient, which of the following effects will gravity have?
Increase the engine power needed to move the vehicle forward.

CD1334

On a gradient, the effect of gravity is to pull the vehicle downhill. For this reason, when travelling uphill, more engine power is required to move the vehicle forward and upward.

Which of the following factors could cause a reduction in a tyre's grip on the road surface?
CD1335
The condition of suspension components.

Grip produces traction, which allows a vehicle to accelerate, change direction and slow down. Understanding the factors which affect grip is critical to safe and effective driving. One such factor is the condition of steering and suspension components.

What should a driver take into account when mounting a tanker?
C0089R
That there may be overhead cables.

If you need to mount the tank of your vehicle, check that the tank is not slippery and that the vehicle is not parked beneath overhead cables. Either of these conditions can cause injury or fatality.

What should a driver be aware of when mounting a tanker?
C7
That the tank might be slippery.

If you need to mount the tank of your vehicle, check that the tank is not slippery and that the vehicle is not parked beneath overhead cables. Either of these conditions can cause injury or fatality.

Carrying Passengers

How many passengers may be carried on a bus?

D0023R

As many as the vehicle's PSV plate specifies.

The maximum number of passengers that may be carried on a bus is specified on the PSV plate. This has implications for the speed limits that apply to the vehicle.

What is the maximum number of adult passengers that a driver who holds a D1 licence may carry in a minibus?

D0024R

16 Passengers.

If you hold a D1 driving licence, you are allowed to drive a bus or coach with a maximum of 16 passenger seats.

What is a bus driver's main responsibility?

D0026RA

The safety and comfort of the passengers.

If you drive a bus, your main responsibility is to ensure the safety and comfort of your passengers. This means delivering them safely to their destination, on time, in a courteous and efficient manner.

What effect could overloading with passengers or goods have on a bus?

It can impair the bus's road-holding ability.

D0028R

Overloading your vehicle can adversely affect the road-holding capabilities of the vehicle. As a bus driver, you are responsible for the safety and comfort of your passengers, and overloading the vehicle puts them at risk.

In what circumstances should the emergency doors be locked when children are being carried on a bus?

D0029R

Never - easy entry and exit from a bus or minibus is essential for safety.

For safety and legal reasons, emergency doors and exits should never be locked when a bus or coach is in service.

Whilst driving a double-decker bus, what should the driver use internal mirrors for? D0031RA

To ensure high standards of passenger care and safety.

Most double-decker buses are fitted with cameras or interior mirrors that are positioned so as to enable the driver to check exits and entrances, stairs and the top deck.

What should a driver do to ensure the safety and comfort of their passengers? D0032R

Drive smoothly and brake evenly.

If you drive a bus, your main responsibility is to ensure the safety and comfort of your passengers. Read the road ahead and plan well in advance for braking and stopping and for changes in direction. This style of driving will help to ensure that your passengers arrive safely at their destinations.

When driving a double-decker bus, how would a driver monitor the passengers on the top deck? D0030R

Frequent use of the internal mirrors and cameras if fitted.

Most double-decker buses are fitted with cameras or interior mirrors that are positioned so as to enable the driver to check exits and entrances, stairs and the top deck.

Whilst driving a double-decker bus, what are the interior mirrors used for? D0031R

Observing passengers who may be standing.

Most double-decker buses are fitted with cameras or interior mirrors that are positioned so as to enable the driver to check exits and entrances, stairs and the top deck.

Why should a driver accelerate smoothly? D0035R

To improve passenger comfort.

If you drive a bus, your main responsibility is to ensure the safety and comfort of your passengers. Read the road ahead and plan well in advance for braking and stopping and for changes in direction. This style of driving will help to ensure that your passengers arrive safely at their destinations.

When letting passengers off the bus, what should a driver do to ensure their safety?
D1

Let the passengers off only when the bus is stopped close to the kerb at a bus stop.

If you drive a bus, your main responsibility is to ensure the safety and comfort of your passengers. Before opening the doors to let them off, make sure that they can alight safely, by checking for other road users, such as pedestrians or cyclists, that may be coming up on the inside.

What driving behaviour could result in passengers getting thrown about?
D0033R

Cornering harshly.

If you drive a bus, your main responsibility is to ensure the safety and comfort of your passengers. Read the road ahead and plan well in advance for braking and stopping and for changes in direction. This style of driving will help to ensure that you brake smoothly and turn at a speed that does not inconvenience or endanger your passengers.

How should a driver show care to the passengers?
D0034R

By allowing them time to get seated.

If you drive a bus, your main responsibility is to ensure the safety and comfort of your passengers. Treat your passengers with care and respect. When you pick up passengers, make sure that they are seated before moving off, and drive in such a way that they are not inconvenienced or endangered. Do not carry more passengers than the vehicle is designed for.

When may a driver carry a passenger on the trailer of a bus?
D0036R

It is never permitted.

Passengers must never be carried in the trailer. If you drive a bus, you are responsible for the safety and comfort of your passengers, and for the vehicle itself. You need to take particular care when towing a trailer, especially when reversing.

Where should passengers' heavy luggage be stored?
D0037R

In the luggage compartment.

If you drive a bus, you are responsible for the safety and comfort of your passengers, and for the vehicle itself. Store heavy luggage in the luggage compartment – if it is in the passenger compartment, it could pose a danger to the passengers in the event of sudden deceleration or change in direction.

What should a driver be aware of before moving off? D0059R
The effect of any sudden movement of the bus on passengers.

Before moving off, braking, stopping or turning, remember that any sudden movement of the vehicle can cause discomfort or danger to passengers, particularly any that are standing or moving around the vehicle.

What should a driver be aware of before moving off from a bus stop? D12A
Persons attempting to get on the bus.

Before moving off, braking, stopping or turning, remember that any sudden movement of the vehicle can cause discomfort or danger to passengers, particularly any that are standing or moving around the vehicle. Before moving off from a bus stop, check the appropriate mirrors to make sure that there is nobody attempting to get on or off.

As a bus driver which of the following may be used to improve customer comfort? RSA01018
Use of appropriate secondary controls.

A professional bus driver must always apply safe driving practices which should include the following: Looking after your passengers (ensuring their safety and comfort).

Which of the following should a professional bus drivers do if there are delays on route? RSA01019
Keep passengers informed.

Depending on the type of bus being driven, for bus and coach companies the driver is the public face of the company and represents the company in its dealings with the passengers.

Private buses and heavy goods first registered after which month and year requires seat belts to be fitted? RSA01020
October 2007

Failure to wear a safety belt is a crime No seat belt, No excuse.

Which of the following skills should a professional bus driver have to deliver excellent customer service? RSA01021
Strong communication skills.

The professional bus driver needs to be able to communicate with a vast number of passengers during the working day. Dealing with all sorts of issues.

What can a bus driver do to avoid harsh braking for the comfort of their passengers?
RSA01022

Read the road ahead and plan early.

For the comfort of all passengers, bus drivers can avoid harsh braking by reading the road ahead, this will allow them to react to the changing traffic situations and brake early to avoid sudden or harsh braking.

When carrying passengers in darkness why should a bus driver have the interior lights switched on in the vehicle?
RSA01024

In order for passengers to move around the bus safely when parked.

When driving a bus in darkness which has passengers aboard, the interior lights must be switched on, this will allow passengers to move around safely and reduce the chances of a passenger tripping or falling.

What should a bus driver do before opening the exit door at a bus stop which is blocked by a parked vehicle?
RSA01025

Check for other road users who may pass on the inside of the bus.

When a bus driver arrives at a passenger stop which is blocked by a parked vehicle, the driver must ensure that there are no other road users such as cyclists passing on the inside of the bus before opening the door to allow passengers on or off the bus.

What is a legal responsibility of bus driver carrying children?
RSA01026

To ensure that passengers under the age of 17 comply with the requirement to wear a seat belt or child restraint.

Make sure passengers aged under 17 use the correct seat, booster seat, booster cushion or seatbelt. All drivers are legally responsible for this. It is an offence to fail to comply with the above outlined child restraint system requirements. Specifically, it is an offence for a driver to allow a person under 17 years of age to occupy a seat without wearing a seatbelt.

Should a driver issue tickets whilst driving away from the bus stop?
RSA01027

No it can be dangerous and the passenger may fall.

It is dangerous to move a bus whilst passengers are not holding on to handle rails.

1

2

Managing Risk

Incidents and Taking Emergency / Corrective Action

What should the driver do if the service brake fails?
CPC1051

Use the secondary brake.

Combine the secondary brake with the foot brake or the parking brake control. This brake is only for use if the service brake fails. As the secondary brake normally operates on fewer wheels than the service brake it is not as effective.

What is the FIRST thing the driver must do if involved in a collision?
CPC1171AA

Stop the vehicle.

Under Irish law, all drivers involved in road traffic collisions firstly must stop their vehicles.

If a vehicle breaks down, where should the driver stop?
CPC1297

As far to the left as possible.

If you break down, try to stop as far to the left as possible to avoid an accident.

What is the most likely cause if a driver is suddenly unable to steer the vehicle properly?
CPC1298A

A front wheel blowout.

A front tyre blowing out or bursting causes the vehicle to suddenly become difficult to steer or control.

Different fire extinguisher types are currently indicated by
CPC1469A

a coloured label.

The coloured plate on new extinguishers tells you the type.

What safety equipment must be carried on a bus or minibus?
D0038R

A fire extinguisher and first aid kit.

All buses or minibuses must carry an advance warning triangle, a fire extinguisher and a first-aid kit. These are the basic essentials that may be needed in an emergency situation, such as a collision.

What should the driver NOT do if a front wheel blows out?
CPC1299A

Swerve quickly to the left.

Do not swerve quickly in any direction until you check that it is safe to change direction. If your front tyre blows out: keep a firm hold on the steering wheel, be aware of anything on your left side, signal left and try to steer a steady course to the left.

By law, what should a driver do if involved in a collision?
CPC1300A

Stop the vehicle.

If you are involved in an accident, you must stop the vehicle and stay at the scene for a reasonable time. This is Irish law.

Hazard warning lights enable a driver to
CPC1301A

warn road users of a vehicle breakdown.

If you arrive at the scene of a breakdown, switch on your hazard warning lights and parking lights. This warns other road users of a breakdown.

In the event of an engine fire where fuel may be involved, what action should be taken?
CPC1302

Spray foam through the grill.

In the case of an engine fire, lifting the bonnet can fan the flames. Water or pressurised carbon dioxide sprayed at a fuel fire will cause it to spread. Use a foam extinguisher to reduce the risk of the fire spreading.

By law, what should a driver do if involved in a collision?
CPC1303A

Stop the vehicle.

If you are involved in an accident, you must stop the vehicle and stay at the scene for a reasonable time. This is Irish law.

What should a driver do if involved in an incident where they feel it was the fault of another driver?
ABMW0612R

Stop immediately and exchange particulars with the other person involved.

If you are involved in any sort of incident with another motorist, you should always exchange insurance details with the other driver and take note of the other vehicle's make and model, colour and registration number. Report the incident to the Gardaí. In a collision where nobody is injured and there is only minor damage to vehicles, the vehicles should be moved to the side of the road to ensure that they do not cause an obstruction or endanger other road users.

If the vehicle breaks down in a tunnel the driver should do any of the following EXCEPT
CPC1304

leave the engine running.

Switch the engine off to reduce the risk of fire. If you break down or crash in a tunnel: switch on the hazard warning lights, switch off the engine, use the emergency phone, check the radio for instructions, check all electronic signs in the tunnel for information.

If a vehicle breaks down on a railway level crossing, what should the driver do?
CPC1305A

Phone the railway controller to alert him/her to the danger.

If you breakdown or get stuck on a level crossing, make sure that everybody gets out and gets clear of the railway line then use the phone provided to contact the signal operator or warn of the danger as best you can.

What is the quickest way to warn other traffic of an accident?
CPC1307

Use hazard lights.

If there is an accident, you should wear a hi-vis vest or jacket and use hazard lights, a torch, beacon and warning triangles to make other road users aware of you and the vehicle. Hazard lights are the quickest way to warn other drivers.

A driver should use hazard warning lights when
CPC1309

a vehicle has broken down.

If you break down, the quickest and easiest way to warn other traffic of the broken down vehicle is to turn on the hazard warning lights.

What should the driver do if a front wheel blows out?
CPC1312A

Keep a firm hold on the wheel.

If your front wheel blows out: keep a tight hold on the steering wheel, be aware of anything on your left side, signal left and try to steer a steady course to the left side, slow down gradually and avoid hard braking, try to stop the vehicle under control.

If the front tyre blows out, what should not be done? CPC1314A
Harsh braking.

Hard and sudden braking will make the vehicle more unstable, so do not do it with reduced road grip. If your front wheel blows out: keep a firm hold on the steering wheel, be aware of anything on your left side, signal left and try to steer a steady course to the left side, slow down gradually and avoid hard braking, try to stop the vehicle under control as far to the left as you can, switch on the hazard warning lights and use a red warning triangle.

When calling for help on an emergency telephone on the motorway, who does the call go to? CPC1317
The Gardaí.

Motorway emergency telephones are free and easy to find. They connect you directly to the Gardaí.

In the event of a breakdown on a motorway, what should be used to identify the location? CPC1320A
Location Reference Indicator (LRI) post.

If you use a mobile phone, identify your location from the marker post (if present) or other clear landmark on the hard shoulder before you phone.

What should the driver do if there is a vehicle fire? CPC1336
Pull over and stop as quickly as possible.

If you think something is wrong with the vehicle, stop as soon as it is safe to do so and assess the situation.

What should a driver do if they think there is a fire inside the engine compartment? CPC1337A
Stop as quickly as possible.

If you think something is wrong with the vehicle, stop as soon as it is safe to do so and assess the situation. If you suspect fire, do not open the engine compartment as the rush of air could fan the flames.

While driving through a tunnel, smoke or fire is noticed in the vehicle, all of the following should be done EXCEPT
CPC1338

stay in the vehicle until help arrives.

Staying in your vehicle may put your safety at risk. If there is smoke or fire in your vehicle: stop your vehicle safely and switch off the engine, leave your vehicle immediately, go to an emergency station and phone the tunnel operator, leave the tunnel from the nearest exit.

While driving through a tunnel with smoke coming from the vehicle in front, the driver should NOT
CPC1339

drive around the smoking vehicle.

If there is smoke or fire in a vehicle in front of you: Stop your vehicle safely and switch off the engine, Leave your vehicle immediately, Go to an emergency station and phone the tunnel operator, Leave the tunnel from the nearest exit. Do not pass.

In the event of vehicle breakdown, the driver should operate the hazard lights then
CPC1396

place a warning triangle behind the vehicle.

Place a warning triangle behind the vehicle and operate the hazard lights if the vehicle is causing an obstruction. Note – some countries do not allow the use of a warning triangle on a motorway.

What should be done in a hi-jack or hostage situation?
CPC1477A

Obey orders.

Do not make the situation worse. Obey any orders given by the person making the threat.

What must a driver do when involved in a collision with another driver where there is minor damage done to the vehicles?
ABMW0614RA

Stop their vehicle and exchange particulars with the driver of the other vehicle.

If you are involved in a collision you must exchange details with the other driver, no matter how minor the damage is. What may look like minor damage at the time may turn out to be more serious when the vehicles are being repaired. Report the incident to the Gardaí.

1
2

Crashes

What is the correct procedure where somebody has been injured in a collision?
ABMW0620RA

Do not move the person unless there is a risk of fire or of the vehicle turning over.

Never move an injured person at the scene of a collision unless there is a risk of fire or further injury. Moving an injured person could make their injuries worse. Call the emergency services (on 999 or 112) or make sure that someone else has called them.

Who should the driver contact when he/she is involved in a collision where another person is injured?
ABMW0622RA

The emergency services.

If you are involved in a collision where someone has been injured, contact the emergency services immediately on 999 or 112. Trained emergency services personnel know best how to attend to injured persons.

In Ireland in 2016, how many road traffic fatalities were there?

151-200
CPC1150BA

This data is taken from 'Road Collision facts 2016' published by the RSA.

About how many vehicles per year hit railway or motorway bridges in Ireland?
CPC1158

185 Vehicles.

This data is taken from 'Road Collision facts 2006' published by the RSA.

Which of these features of a vehicle is MOST likely to cause an accident?

Vehicle width.
CPC1164

Wide vehicles may obstruct other drivers' views and need extra space for turning. On narrow roads they also make it difficult for other vehicles to remain on the road.

What is the estimated cost, including lost output, human costs, medical cost, property loss, insurance, and policing, of a road death in Ireland?

CPC1182

€2,667,000

Estimated cost reported to and recorded by An Garda Síochana in 2006.

What is the estimated cost, including lost output, human costs, medical cost, property loss, insurance, and policing, of a minor road injury in Ireland?

CPC1184

€35,000

This data is taken from 'Road Collision facts 2006' published by the RSA.

The first person on the scene of an accident should call 999.

CPC1316

If you arrive at the scene of an accident, call for help on 999 or 112. If the first person does this, help may arrive sooner.

1
2

When should an injured person be moved?

CPC1322

If the person needs CPR.

Do not move an injured person unless there is a serious risk of fire or explosion.

When dealing with accident victims, remember A B C. What does A stand for?

CPC1324

Airway.

Remember A B C: Airway – clear the airway and keep open, Breathing – check if they are breathing and make sure they keep breathing, Circulation – check pulse and stop severe bleeding, give CPR if needed.

When dealing with accident victims, remember A B C. What does C stand for?

CPC1326

Circulation.

Remember A B C: Airway – clear the airway and keep open, Breathing – check if they are breathing and make sure they keep breathing, Circulation – check pulse and stop severe bleeding, give CPR if needed.

What is the best first aid for a person who has been burned?
CPC1329
Apply cold water to the burn.

Check the person for shock, then try to cool the burn if you can. Try to find water or other liquid that is clean, cold and non-toxic to pour on it. The cool liquid may cool the affected area down and reduce damage.

At an accident scene, which of these is NOT a sign of shock?
CPC1330
Bleeding.

The effects of shock may not be obvious. Look for warning signs such as rapid pulse, pale grey skin, sweating and rapid shallow breathing. Bleeding is a sign of other injury.

If an arm or leg is bleeding but not broken, what should be done?
CPC1331
Raise arm or leg to reduce blood flow.

If an arm or leg is bleeding but not broken, raise it to reduce the flow of blood.

When dealing with accident victims, remember A B C. What does B stand for?
CPC1333
Breathing.

Remember A B C: Airway – clear the airway and keep open, Breathing – check if they are breathing and make sure they keep breathing, Circulation – check pulse and stop severe bleeding, give CPR if needed.

At the scene of an accident, the drivers involved must exchange all of the following information EXCEPT
CPC1354
age of the vehicles.

If you are involved in an accident you must give your name and address, the address where the vehicle is kept, the name and address of the vehicle owner, the vehicle's registration number and evidence of insurance. You do not have to give information about the age of the vehicle at the scene of an accident (other than its vehicle registration number).

How many road deaths were there in Ireland in 2012?
CPC1409B
162.

In 2006, there were 365 road deaths in Ireland. This number continues to fall thanks to the improved behaviour of all road users. By taking personal responsibility for your own behaviour on the roads, you can help further improve these figures.

Driving with anticipation and awareness can result in a reduced accident risk.

CPC1461

By driving with anticipation and awareness of surroundings, you reduce your risk of being involved in an accident.

If a driver is involved in a collision, when should they inform their insurance company?

ABMW0613R

As soon as they possibly can.

If you are involved in an incident with another vehicle, you should inform your insurance company as soon as possible. This will help with any claims that may be made by another party against your insurance company.

What should a driver do if involved in an incident where there is damage to property only?

ABMW0615R

It is not necessary to report it to the Gardai provided it has been reported to the property owner.

If you are involved in an incident where the only damage is to property (for example, a garden wall or fence or a parked car), you must report it to the owner or to the person in charge of the property, or to the Gardaí if nearby. If you cannot do his, you should report the incident to a Garda station as soon as possible.

What should a driver do where a person has been injured in a collision?

Move the victim only if there is a risk of fire or further injury.

ABMW0616R

Never move an injured person at the scene of a collision unless there is a risk of fire or further injury. Moving an injured person could add to their injuries. Trained personnel know best how to attend to injured persons. Call the emergency services (on 999 or 112) or make sure that someone else has called them.

What type of drink should be given to a person who has been injured in a collision?

ABMW0617R

No drink should be given.

A person who has been injured in a collision should not be given anything to drink, as this could cause them to choke. Only trained personnel should attend to an injured person. Call the emergency services (on 999 or 112) or make sure that someone else has called them.

What should a driver do to assist a person who is unconscious following a collision?
ABMW0618R

Loosen tight clothing around the neck and keep the person warm with a blanket or overcoat.

If a person is unconscious following a collision, you should loosen tight clothing around the their neck and keep them warm with a blanket or overcoat until the emergency services arrive. Call the emergency services (on 999 or 112) or make sure that someone else has called them.

Who should first be contacted where a person has been injured in a collision?
ABMW0621R

The emergency services.

Where somebody has been injured in a collision, it is important to call the emergency services immediately on 999 or 112. Trained emergency services personnel know best how to attend to injured persons.

If a driver is involved in a collision with an uninsured visiting motorist, where nobody is injured, who should it be reported to?
ABMW0623R

The driver's insurance company and the Gardai.

If you are involved in any type of collision, you should always report it to the Gardai and to your insurance company.

What should a driver do if involved in a collision with another vehicle where nobody is injured?
ABMW0624R

Exchange all relevant details with the other driver and report it to the Gardai.

If a you are involved in a collision with another vehicle where nobody is injured, you should exchange all the relevant details with the other driver – including name, address, vehicle registration, make and model and all insurance details.

What should a driver do if they arrive at the scene of a collision involving a vehicle carrying hazardous materials?
ABMW0625R

Keep well clear and raise the alarm.

If you arrive at the scene of a collision involving a vehicle carrying hazardous materials, you should keep well clear of the scene. Call the emergency services on 999 or 112 and give them as much information as you can about the marking labels on the vehicle. You should also warn other road users about the danger.

Load Handling

How many road deaths were there in Ireland in 2012?   CPC1409B
162.

In 2006, there were 365 road deaths in Ireland. This number continues to fall thanks to the improved behaviour of all road users. By taking personal responsibility for your own behaviour on the roads, you can help further improve these figures.

When handling a load, where on the driver's body should the load be positioned?   CPC1226AA
Waist.

Keep the load and your arms close to the waist. Hug it close to the body if you can. This may help to reduce the risk of injury.

When lifting a load, the driver should have   CPC1227A
feet apart, with one leg slightly forward of the other.

Place your feet about hip distance apart with one leg slightly forward to help keep your balance. This may help to reduce the risk of injury.

When starting to lift, what is the best position for a driver's back?   CPC1228
Straight but inclined forward.

Keeping the normal curve of your back while lifting may help to reduce the risk of injury.

If a driver needs to turn when handling a heavy package, he/she should   CPC1229AA
move with the feet.

Move with your feet, not your waist. Turn feet in the direction of the move. This may help to reduce the risk of injury.

On an uneven surface using a well-maintained handling aid, up to what percentage of the load weight may be needed to move a load? CPC1243
10%

You need more force to move objects over an uneven surface. Depending on how uneven the surface is and the size of the wheels on a moving cart, the force needed to start the load moving could be up to 10% of the load.

When handling goods the main risk of injury is wear and tear to the back. CPC1440

The main concern with manual handling is the increased risk of injury due to wear and tear on your back.

The science of fitting the job to the worker is known as CPC1441
ergonomics.

The RST-CMT-08, CPC Manual defines ergonomics as "the science of fitting the job to the worker and adapting the work environment to the needs of humans."

The first step in lifting safely is to CPC1442
assess the load.

To make a safe and successful lift, you should first assess the load and determine the load's weight, its edges and surface, then decide how to hold it.

Protective Clothing

A driver should wear protective clothing, including gloves when refueling. CPC1244

Fuel is a toxic substance which can splash or spill when you fuel a vehicle. Wear protective clothing and gloves to help prevent contact with skin.

Who is responsible for supplying any Personal Protective Equipment required by the driver? CD1303
The employer.

The regulations require employers to provide personal protective equipment to their employees where there is a risk to their health and safety.

To ensure that Personal Protective Equipment is maintained in serviceable condition, it should be inspected CD1304
before initial use during each work shift.

The regulations require that personal protective equipment is serviceable and fit for purpose. Regular inspections ensure that this equipment is maintained in this condition.

Personal Protective Equipment that is found to be defective or damaged on inspection must be repaired or replaced CD1305
before initial use during each work shift.

The regulations require that personal protective equipment is serviceable and fit for purpose whenever it is required. As such, if it is found to be defective, it should be replaced or repaired before work begins.

1
2

Weather Related Matters

In icy or frosty conditions, drivers should allow up to ten times the normal distance for braking.
CPC1125A

Explanation: Ice and frost greatly reduce tyre-to-road surface traction. Allow up to ten times the usual distance for braking to help compensate for the loss of traction.

A lightness in the steering MOST likely indicates ice.
CPC1138A

Lightness in steering indicates a loss of traction. Ice provides a harder, smoother surface than rain, or snow so it is difficult to avoid skidding.

When driving in heavy rain, what should a driver do?
Switch the windscreen wipers on to high and drive at a reduced speed.
CD14

When driving in the rain, your visibility can be severely reduced both by the rain itself and by the spray thrown up by other road users. Stopping distances on wet roads are greater than on dry, and you should reduce speed accordingly.

Why should spray suppression equipment be fitted to a large vehicle?
To reduce the amount of water sprayed up from the wheels.
CD0086R

When a vehicle is driven on a wet road, its wheels throw up spray, and this has the potential to reduce visibility for other drivers. A spray suppression system generally includes mudguards, rain flaps and wheel skirts designed to reduce the amount of spray generated by a vehicle. A driver should check the spray suppression equipment on the vehicle before setting out on a journey, especially in bad weather.

What should a driver do before starting a journey in bad weather?
Check the weather forecast for the planned route.
CD0099AA

Driving in bad weather is more dangerous and more tiring. You should check the weather forecast and other sources for information on the expected conditions on the intended route, and allow extra time to complete the journey.

122

What should a driver ensure when driving a diesel engined vehicle in cold weather?

CD0101R

That winter-grade fuel is used.

In extremely cold weather, diesel fuel is liable to freeze, particularly in the fuel lines. To prevent this, in winter you should use diesel fuel that has had an anti-waxing agent added to it.

How should a descent be negotiated in snow or frosty weather?

CD0103

Engage a lower gear and use gentle braking applications to keep the speed down.

In snow or ice, a vehicle takes longer to stop. Before starting a descent in a large vehicle in such conditions, reduce speed and select a lower gear. Brake gently and only when needed. If the vehicle is fitted with a manually selectable retarder, engage it before starting the descent.

1

2

When driving in heavy rain, what should a driver do?

CD0102R

Drive at a slower speed to allow for reduced visibility and increased braking distance.

When driving in the rain, your visibility can be severely reduced both by the rain itself and by the spray thrown up by other road users. Stopping distances on wet roads are greater than on dry, and you should reduce speed accordingly.

What should a driver do when overtaking a vehicle which is displacing mud and spray?

CD0104R

Use the vehicle windscreen wipers and washer system.

In wet weather, vehicles tend to throw up spray and mud, and this can affect visibility for other road users. Before starting a journey make sure that the windscreen wipers are working and the washer reservoir is topped up. Then use these systems as necessary to clear the windscreen, especially when overtaking other vehicles.

What should a driver do when overtaking a large vehicle that is throwing up spray? CD0105R

Move out earlier than normal and give extra clearance.

In wet weather, vehicles tend to throw up spray and mud, and this can affect visibility for other road users. To minimize this danger, read the road ahead, and when overtaking move out earlier than usual, giving the vehicle you are overtaking extra clearance. This will reduce the amount of spray being deposited on your windscreen.

What should a driver do before starting a journey in bad weather?

Check the weather forecast for the planned route. CD0149RA

Before you leave your vehicle, apply the handbrake and switch off the ignition. Remember to secure the vehicle by closing windows and locking all doors.

In wet weather how might a driver judge what is a safe following distance from the vehicle in front? ABMW0428R

By allowing at least four seconds to elapse between the vehicle in front and the driver's own vehicle passing a fixed point.

In wet conditions you should maintain a gap of at least four seconds from the vehicle in front – twice as long as in dry conditions.

Vision & Visibility

How can sunlight affect visibility in a vehicle with grimy windows?

It can create a mirror effect and reduce visibility. CD0140

When driving in sunny weather all the vehicle's windows should be clean. A grimy or greasy windscreen can impair your ability to see the road ahead and compromise your ability to react and respond to changing conditions.

When driving a large vehicle, what is the most effective way for the driver to ensure that they can see to the side and rear of the vehicle?

Making full use of exterior mirrors. CD0141R

When driving a large vehicle you should make full use of your exterior mirrors so that you are constantly aware of what is happening around you, and that you can react and respond appropriately.

1

2

How can the height of the cab affect the driver's ability to see other road users? CD0143R

A high cab can make it more difficult to see pedestrians and cyclists adjacent to the cab.

In a high cab it can be more difficult to see pedestrians and cyclists that are adjacent to the cab. They may be out of sight below the windscreen line and/or side window line. Blind-spot mirrors should be fitted and should be used particularly when moving off and in slow-moving traffic.

What should a driver do when the exterior mirrors are covered with a film of dirt or grime? CD0144R

Stop the vehicle and clean the mirrors before continuing.

A driver should always ensure that they can see clearly in their exterior mirrors. If you discover that your mirrors are dusty or dirty, you should clean them before continuing so that you have maximum visibility of the road around you.

Which of the following can a driver do to control the risk of being dazzled when driving into a low sun? CD1336

Keep the inside of the windscreen clean.

Drivers can be dazzled when driving into a low sun. The build-up of a film of dirt on the inside of the windscreen can make it even harder to see when driving into a low sun. Keeping the inside of the windscreen clean can help avoid the risk of being dazzled.

Which of the following can a driver do to help make driving in fog safer? CD1337

Drive slowly and steadily.

Fog is usually patchy and you will pass through areas where visibility varies. Don't be tempted to speed up through the good patches, as you might find yourself suddenly in another dense patch. Driving at a steady, slow speed helps to manage this risk.

The 'mist up' of windows that can be experienced when driving in heavy rain is caused by CD1338

the contrast in temperatures on the inside and outside of the windows.

When driving in heavy rain the 'mist up' of windows further reduces visibility. Understanding the factors which cause this mist up can enable the driver to manage this situation.

During normal visibility conditions during daylight which of the following lights does the RSA recommend using? CD1339

Dipped headlights.

RSA recommends the use of daytime running lights (where fitted) or dipped headlights during daylight conditions.

When driving in a poorly lit area at night, how can a driver avoid dazzling oncoming traffic? CD1340

Switch to dipped headlights.

When travelling in a poorly lit area at night, dipped headlights help to avoid dazzling an oncoming driver.

A driver is preparing to undertake a journey at night and discovers that dense fog is forecast. How can the driver BEST minimise risk in this situation? CD1341

Postpone the journey.

If fog becomes thick at night, and a large vehicle is unable to proceed safely, it may become a serious hazard to other traffic. For this reason, if thick fog is forecast at night, it is better not to start out in the first instance.

What should a driver do if dazzled by the lights of an oncoming vehicle? ABMW0266R

Look to the left-hand edge of the roadway and if necessary reduce speed.

If you are dazzled by the lights of oncoming traffic, turn your eyes to the left edge of the road. If necessary, stop and allow your eyes to recover before driving on.

1
2

What should a driver do before towing a wide-bodied trailer? BW0006R

Make use of extended mirrors to check for following traffic.

If you intend towing a trailer that is wider or higher than the vehicle that is towing it, you should fit extended mirrors to both sides of the towing vehicle, so that you will be able to assess the traffic situation behind and to the sides.

What specific observations should a driver make before reversing a vehicle fitted with an audible warning device? BW0013

Observations should be made to the front, sides and rear of the vehicle, including blind spots.

Before reversing, make sure it is safe to do so by taking all appropriate observations to the front, sides and rear of the vehicle, including the blind spots. Never assume it is safe to reverse just because the vehicle has an audible warning device.

Alighting from the Vehicle

When letting passengers out of your vehicle, or when getting out yourself, you should make sure that you are doing so safely, and that you are not putting other road users in danger.

What precaution should a driver take when allowing passengers to alight from a bus or minibus? CD0152RA

Make sure that the passengers exit on the side away from the centre of the road.

Before allowing passengers off the bus, you should stop close to the kerb on the left to allow passengers an easy and safe exit from the vehicle.

How should a driver get out of a truck cab? C0085R

Use the step and handrails provided while facing towards the cab.

To safely exit the cab of a truck, first check whether it is safe to do so, and then climb down facing towards the cab, using the handrails for support.

If a driver comes to a halt in stationary traffic in a tunnel, what should they do? CD0159R

Switch off the engine.

If, when driving a large vehicle through a tunnel, you are halted in stationary traffic for any length of time, you should switch off the engine to reduce fumes in the tunnel and conserve fuel.

If a vehicle being driven through a tunnel breaks down, what should the driver do? CD0160R

Call for help from an emergency station.

If, when driving a large vehicle through a tunnel, your vehicle breaks down or is involved in an incident, switch on the hazard warning lights, switch off the engine, and use the emergency phone at the emergency station to call for help.

If a vehicle being driven through a tunnel breaks down, what should the driver do?
CD0161R

Use the emergency telephone to call for help.

If, when driving a large vehicle through a tunnel, your vehicle breaks down or is involved in an incident, switch on the hazard warning lights, switch off the engine, and use the emergency phone at the emergency station to call for help.

If a vehicle being driven through a tunnel breaks down, what should the driver do?
CD0162R

Switch on the hazard warning lights.

If, when driving a large vehicle through a tunnel, your vehicle breaks down or is involved in an incident, switch on the hazard warning lights, switch off the engine, and use the emergency phone at the emergency station to call for help.

If a vehicle being driven through a tunnel goes on fire, what should the driver do?
CD0163R

Leave the vehicle immediately and use the emergency phone at the nearest emergency station.

If, when driving a large vehicle through a tunnel, a fire breaks out in your vehicle, switch off the engine, leave the vehicle immediately, use the emergency phone at the emergency station to alert the tunnel operator, and leave the tunnel at the nearest available exit.

A vehicle strikes a railway bridge. When reporting the incident, the driver must give all of the following information EXCEPT
CPC1356

the height of the vehicle.

Under Irish law, you must report any bridge strike. Your report must include the location, the damage and bridge reference number. You do not need to report vehicle height but you must know the height of your vehicle.

When leaving the cab of a bus, what should the driver ensure?
D9

That the engine is switched off.

When parking a bus, you should make sure that it is in a safe place, the parking brake is on, the engine is switched off, and the electrical master switch is off. Before leaving the cab, check for approaching traffic to make sure it is safe to disembark.

What should a driver check before moving off after dropping off passengers?
D0027R

Both exterior mirrors.

Before moving off, check your off-side exterior mirror for overtaking traffic and other road users and your nearside exterior mirror for intending passengers rushing to catch the bus. Check these mirrors as many times as necessary.

How should a driver exit the cab of a bus with the driver's door on the offside?
D0039R

By climbing down while facing inwards.

When getting out of the cab of a bus that has the driver's door on the off-side, face inwards, so that you can climb down safely in a gradual manner.

When should the passenger door be opened on a bus or minibus?
D0040R

When stopped at a place where it is safe for passengers to get out.

You should allow passengers to get on and off the bus only when it is stopped in a safe place. This (apart from emergencies) is the only situation in which the passenger door should be opened.

When leaving the cab of a bus, what should a driver ensure?
D0052R

That the parking brake is on.

When parking a bus, you should make sure that it is in a safe place, the parking brake is on, the engine is switched off, and the electrical master switch is off. Before leaving the cab, check for approaching traffic to make sure it is safe to disembark.

When leaving the cab of a bus, what should the driver ensure?
D0053R

That the electrical master switch is off.

When parking a bus, you should make sure that it is in a safe place, the parking brake is on, the engine is switched off, and the electrical master switch is off. Before leaving the cab, check for approaching traffic to make sure it is safe to disembark.

When children are alighting from a school bus, what advice should a driver give them?
D0041R

To stay well in off the road until the bus has moved away.

If you drive a bus, your main responsibility is to ensure the safety and comfort of your passengers. Schoolchildren in particular can be excitable, unruly and unpredictable. When passengers are getting off the bus, advise them to stay off the road until the bus has moved away, and check that the road is clear behind and to the sides before moving off.

What should a driver do when wishing to stop to allow passengers to get off the bus?
D0042R

Stop where the passengers getting off the bus will not be in danger from other traffic.

You should allow passengers to get on and off the bus only when it is stopped in a safe place where they will not be in danger from other traffic or in a position where their footing may be undermined.

In relation to the passenger doors, what in particular should a driver be aware of when driving a bus?

That the passenger doors should be locked.
D0043RA

For safety and legal reasons, emergency doors and exits should never be locked when a bus or coach is in service.

Which of the following sequences of action should a driver follow to safely exit a cab?

Open door - face vehicle - grab the handhold - step down backwards.
C1312

To safely exit the cab of a truck, a driver should face towards the cab and climb down, using the handholds for support.

Which of the following driver behaviours help to ensure a safe exit from the cab?

Using the proper handholds.
C1313

Using the proper handholds supports the driver when climbing down from a cab, helping to ensure a safe exit.

Driving in Tunnels

Before driving through a tunnel, what should a driver do? CD0153R
Check that the height of the vehicle is less than the signed limit.

If your route takes you through a tunnel, you must make sure in advance that your vehicle does not exceed the height limit for the tunnel. If your vehicle is higher than the limit displayed on the tunnel height-limit sign, you must take an alternative route.

Before driving through a tunnel, what should a driver do? CD0154RA
Check the tunnel height before starting the journey.

If your route takes you through a tunnel, you must make sure in advance that your vehicle does not exceed the height limit for the tunnel. If your vehicle is higher than the limit displayed on the tunnel height-limit sign, you must take an alternative route.

When driving through a tunnel, what should a driver do? CD0157R
Maintain a safe distance from the vehicle in front.

When entering a tunnel in a large vehicle, slow down and allow a 100-metre gap between your vehicle and the vehicle in front. Because of its size, your vehicle might make it more difficult for following traffic to see the road ahead.

If there is unexpected traffic congestion in a tunnel, what should a driver do? CD0158R
Switch on hazard warning lights.

If, when driving a large vehicle through a tunnel, you meet traffic congestion, leave a safe distance between you and the vehicle in front and switch on your hazard warning lights when stationary.

Vehicle Safety Equipment

1

2

133

Vehicle Safety Equipment

Who is responsible for ensuring that a child wears a child restraint system in a vehicle?
BW0123A

The driver

If the passenger is over the age of 17, it is their responsibility to comply with the seat belt regulations. Below that age, it is the driver's responsibility.

What colour rear markings must be fitted to a category C type vehicle?
C0083R

Red reflector stripes.

All category C type vehicles must have reflective markings on the sides and rear. The markings on the rear of the vehicle must be red; those on the sides can be white or amber.

What is the purpose of rear under-run barriers?
C0084

To prevent cars from going under the body of the vehicle from the rear.

Rear under-run barriers are protection barriers attached to the rear of a truck, trailer or semi-trailer. They are designed to prevent small vehicles such as cars and light vans from going under the truck if it stops or decelerates suddenly, and thus help to avoid or reduce serious or fatal injury.

What colour of retro reflective material should be used on the rear of vehicles?
C1328A

Red

The rear and side vehicle markings should be made of strips of Retro Reflective Material.

A rear underrun protective device is required on goods vehicles, trailers, and semi-trailers exceeding what Maximum Authorised Mass?
C1329

3,500 kg.

Goods vehicles and trailers having a design gross vehicle weight exceeding 3,500 kg must be fitted with a rear underrun protective device.

Which of the following rear underrun protective devices would pass a vehicle inspection?
C1330

The distance between the device and the road surface is 550mm.

Rear underrun protective devices must not increase the overall width of the vehicle when fitted.

Who is responsible for ensuring that a passenger over 17 years of age is wearing a seat belt while travelling in a car? BW0121R
The passenger only.

If the passenger is over the age of 17, it is their responsibility to comply with the seat belt regulations. Below that age, it is the driver's responsibility.

Who is responsible for ensuring that a passenger under 17 years of age is wearing a seat belt while travelling in a car? BW0122R
The driver only.

If the passenger is over the age of 17, it is their responsibility to comply with the seat belt regulations. Below that age, it is the driver's responsibility.

In general, how should infants be secured in a vehicle? BW0124
They should always be secured in a child restraint system.

As safety belts are designed mainly for adults and older children, infants and small children must be restrained in an appropriate child restraint system.

Should an infant who is not secured in a child restraint system be carried in the front passenger seat? BW0125R
No, an infant must always be restrained in a correct child seat.

Infants and small children must be restrained in an appropriate child restraint system.

How should a child restraint system be secured in a vehicle? BW0126R
It should be secured with seat belts or ISOFIX fittings.

A child restraint system should be secured in the vehicle either with the seatbelts of the car or with approved fixings. Always use a restraint system that is appropriate for the age, height and weight of the child, and follow the manufacturer's instructions.

What should a driver do when driving a vehicle with young children as passengers? BW0127R
Make sure each child is wearing a seat belt or using an appropriate restraint system.

If the passenger is over the age of 17, it is their responsibility to comply with the seatbelt regulations. Below that age, it is the driver's responsibility.

What is the purpose of side-impact protection bars?
To protect the occupants when the vehicle is hit from the side. BW0128

Side-impact protection bars are fitted to some vehicles to protect the occupants of the vehicle in the event of a collision from the side.

Socially Responsible Driving

Fitness to Drive

What can make a driver feel sleepy?
CPC0232

Eating a large meal.

Don't drive after a heavy meal as it may make you sleepy.

After driving for four hours and feeling sleepy, what is the best action a driver can take to avoid an accident?
CPC1172

Stop and drink 2 cups of strong coffee and have a nap.

Stopping to take a nap for 15 minutes after drinking a caffeinated drink such as tea, coffee or cola, may allow you to drive for as much as another hour.

What could badly affect a driver's reactions, especially in an emergency?
Feeling tired.
CPC1231

Many studies show that when you are tired you don't react as quickly.

An applicant may be refused a Category C or D driving licence if he/she suffered a stroke within the last
CPC1239

1 year.

Drivers must meet basic health and fitness standards. You may be refused a PCV or HGV driving licence if you have suffered a stroke within the past year.

What type of food does the body digest slowly so one doesn't feel hungry?
CPC1262

Pasta.

Meals based around slowly digested carbohydrates such as Pasta, bread, rice, and vegetables will keep you fuller for longer than food high in sugar, which gives you immediate energy but makes you feel hungry sooner.

What type of food does the body digest slowly so one doesn't feel hungry?
CPC1265

Bread.

Meals based around slowly digested carbohydrates such as bread, rice, pasta, and vegetables will keep you fuller for longer than those high in sugar. This may help you to concentrate.

In case of delays, what is the best drink to carry on a journey?

CPC1266

Water.

You should carry water in case of delays on your journey, especially in summer. Water is the ideal drink. It quenches thirst for longer than drinks such as coffee or tea, which can make you need the toilet more often. This can be important if you drive long distances between breaks.

What food is high in protein?

CPC1268

Fish.

Meals based around protein-rich foods, such as meat, fish, eggs, cheese and peas or beans, will keep you fuller for longer. Protein foods may help you to concentrate as you will not feel hungry for a longer period.

What drink quenches thirst for longer than any other?

CPC1269

Water.

Water is the ideal drink. It quenches your thirst for longer than drinks such as coffee or tea, which can make you need the toilet more often.

What food is high in protein?

CPC1271

Eggs.

Meals based around protein-rich foods, such as eggs, meat, fish, cheese, and peas or beans, will keep you fuller for longer and may help you to concentrate.

For how long may some drugs remain in the body?

CPC1278

Up to 72 hours.

The effects of alcohol last about 24 hours. Many drugs remain in the body for up to 72 hours.

It is an offence for a professional driver of a bus or truck to drive such a vehicle when that driver's blood alcohol level is above

CPC1279A

20 mg per 100 ml.

The current legal limit in Ireland is a blood alcohol content (BAC) of 0.8 g per litre (80 mg per 100 ml). This is the legal limit in 3 of 25 EU-member states. Your crash risk increases with a higher BAC and the crashes become more severe.

If tired, how long of a nap could allow a driver another hour of driving time? CPC1282A
15 minutes.

You can do a number of things to stop you feeling sleepy while driving. Eating a heavy meal will make you sleepy.

All of the following will help to avoid tiredness while driving EXCEPT
eating a heavy meal before the journey. CPC1283

If you feel tiredness coming on, open the windows, turn the heating down and get off the motorway. A heavy meal, a warm cab, the constant drone of the engine and long unbroken stretches of road, especially at night, can make you sleepy.

What will most likely help a driver to stay awake while driving at night?
Taking planned rest breaks. CPC1284

If you drive alone, play the radio, chew gum or talk. Plan a break at least every two hours or every 100 miles.

Driving at night on a motorway with warm air inside the vehicle could
make the driver feel sleepy. CPC1287A

Signs that you are tired include sleepiness, slowed reactions and impaired judgement.
An 'alert' reaction is not a symptom of tiredness.

Which of these is NOT a symptom of tiredness? CPC1455
Alert reactions.

A number of factors can contribute to a driver becoming tired. One of these is poor driving conditions.

What may cause a driver to feel tired when driving?
Poor driving conditions.

In moving traffic, keep a safe distance by staying at least two seconds behind the vehicle in front. This is known as the two-second rule. In wet weather, double this distance.

What effect does drinking alcohol have on a driver?
ABMW0389R
It makes the driver drowsy.

Alcohol is a major factor in collisions that lead to death and injury. Even small amounts of alcohol affect your judgement, your concentration and your ability to react to hazards. A driver should never ever drink and drive.

If a motorist or a motorcyclist is taking medication which may affect their driving, what should they do?
ABMW0390R
Seek medical advice in relation to driving.

Some medication can affect a driver's ability to drive safely. If you are on medication of any kind, you should ask your doctor or pharmacist to tell you if it is safe to drive while taking it. Read the patient information leaflet supplied with the medication.

1

2

Control of Vehicle

A loss of grip between the tyre and the road surface can most likely be caused by
CPC1315
sudden acceleration.

Friction is the grip between two surfaces. This friction is reduced when you accelerate suddenly. The grip the tyres have on the road surface transmits the force (traction) you need when moving away or accelerating, turning or changing directions, and braking.

When adjusting the driver's seat, the driver needs to ensure which of the following?
CD1343
They can reach the pedals easily.

The driver's seat should be adjusted such that the driver is comfortable, has good visibility and can reach the pedals and hand controls easily.

To ensure an ergonomically sound driving position, drivers should ensure which of the following are adjusted comfortably?
CD1345
Mirrors.

All mirrors should be adjusted so that they can be viewed correctly and without strain.

A driver experiences aching shoulders, arms and back after a long drive. This may indicate which of the following?
CD1346
Poor posture.

A poor driving position and posture may cause a driver to experience aching shoulders, arms and back after a long drive.

Tyre pressure should be maintained to which of the following specifications for large or high sided vehicles?
CD1348
Per the manufacturer's recommendation.

Tyres must be maintained at the correct pressure. The appropriate pressure differs across different types and models of tyre, so manufacturers' recommendations should be followed for the correct pressure required.

Anticipation and Reaction

What is the MOST likely cause of multiple pile-ups on motorways?
Driving too close.   CPC1139

Because you travel at faster speeds on motorways, driving too close to other vehicles gives you less time to respond safely.

What is the minimum safe distance between vehicles when weather conditions are good?   CPC1346
A two second gap.

The link between pedestrian deaths and vehicle speed is based on research by the Royal Society for the Prevention of Accidents. Death rates may be higher where a pedestrian is hit by a large vehicle.

A driver who is tailgating is   CD1359
following the vehicle ahead too closely.

Tailgating means you are following dangerously close behind another vehicle, at speed, with maybe only a few feet apart. It often happens on motorways.

What is the correct action to take in this situation?   ABMW0222R
Keep a close eye on children. If necessary give a warning signal and be prepared to brake in good time.

Because it is difficult to predict children's behaviour, you should always be prepared to react to a change in the traffic situation or to stop.

An approaching driver notices that the boy on the children's bicycle has said goodbye to his friend. What is the correct action for the driver to take?   ABMW0223R
Be prepared for the boy setting off at any moment without paying attention to your vehicle.

Because it is difficult to predict children's behaviour, you should always be prepared to react to a change in the traffic situation or to stop.

When approaching the pedestrian crossing, what should the driver do in this situation?
ABMW0227R

Slow down in good time and be prepared to stop.

When there are pedestrians at or near a zebra crossing, you should slow down on approach and be prepared to stop to allow the pedestrians to cross safely.

What should a driver be alert to in this area?
ABMW0231R

Pedestrians may cross between parked cars.

When driving in a built-up area, you should drive with caution and be prepared to react to pedestrians crossing from between parked vehicles.

1

2

What should the driver do if there are children playing at the edge of the roadway?
ABMW0232R

Reduce speed, drive cautiously and remain ready to brake.

Because it is difficult to predict children's behaviour, you should always be prepared to react to a change in the traffic situation and be prepared to stop.

The silver car is overtaking the parked red car, what should the driver do in this situation?
ABMW0237R

Reduce speed considerably and be ready to stop.

You should read the road and be extra careful while driving through an area where children might be playing. When a ball bounces out on the road you should expect that a child might follow to retrieve the ball.

What should a driver be aware of in this situation?
ABMW0238R

Pedestrians may leave the traffic island without paying attention.

You should read the road ahead and expect extra pedestrian activity when the tram is at the stop.

What should the driver be most conscious of in this situation?
ABMW0248R

The pedestrian may suddenly cross the road in front of the vehicle.

It is often difficult to predict other road users' behaviour. Where there are parked vehicles on both sides of the road you should approach with caution, and be prepared to react to a change in the traffic situation and to stop.

What should the driver do when approaching this situation?
ABMW0249R

Reduce speed and remain ready to brake since the girl on foot could suddenly cross the road.

It is often difficult to predict other road users' behaviour. You should be prepared in case the pedestrian steps onto the road and the silver car stops suddenly.

What should a driver be aware of in this situation?
ABMW0252R

The cyclist will move onto the roadway without paying attention to moving traffic.

You should show extra care when approaching cyclists who are about to exit from a cycle lane and join the roadway.

What does a continuous white line along the centre of the road mean? ABMW0256R
No U-turn allowed.

You must never do a U-turn on any stretch of road with a continuous white line along its centre. The restricted vision at such places would make doing a U-turn very unsafe.

How should a driver overtake the cyclist in this situation? ABMW0257R
By crossing the broken white line.

Where there are two lines in the centre of the road, you must obey the one closest to you. So, if the closest line is a broken white line, by law you may overtake, so long as it is safe to do so.

What does a white line in the centre of the road mean? ABMW0259R
Vehicles may not cross or straddle the line.

You must not cross or straddle a continuous white line in the centre of the road unless you wish to enter land or premises and it is safe to do so.

Why might it be dangerous to drive on a poorly-lit street? ABMW0262R
Pedestrians crossing in a dark area might be difficult to see.

When you are driving along a poorly-lit street, you should take extra care – vulnerable road users such as pedestrians might not be so easy to see. You should always be prepared to react to a change in the traffic situation.

Why might it be dangerous to drive on a poorly-lit street?
ABMW0263R

It may be difficult to make out poorly lit vehicles in the dark areas.

When you are driving along a poorly-lit street, you should take extra care and be prepared to react to hazards such as unlit parked vehicles.

What danger should a driver allow for over the brow of this hill?
ABMW0272R

There may be a slow moving vehicle in your lane.

On the approach to the brow of a hill you should be extra careful and be prepared to react to a change in the traffic situation.

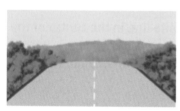

What danger should a driver allow for over the brow of this hill?
ABMW0273R

A vehicle may be broken down.

On the approach to the brow of a hill you should be extra careful and be prepared to react to a change in the traffic situation.

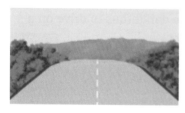

What danger should a driver allow for over the brow of this hill?
ABMW0275R

There may be oncoming pedestrians.

On the approach to the brow of a hill you should be extra careful and be prepared to react to a change in the traffic situation.

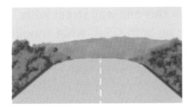

What danger should a driver allow for over the brow of this hill?
ABMW0276R

There may be livestock on the road.

On approach to the brow of a hill you should be extra careful and be prepared to react to a change in the traffic situation.

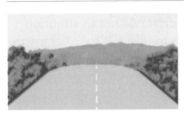

What danger should a driver allow for over the brow of this hill?
ABMW0277R

There may be hedge-cutting taking place.

On the approach to the brow of a hill you should be extra careful and be prepared to react to a change in the traffic situation.

What should a driver be aware of when following the motorcyclist, and the white car is reversing onto the road?
ABMW0282R

The driver following the motorcycle may need a longer braking distance than normal.

You should always keep a safe distance from the vehicle in front if it is slowing down or stopping. Always read the road and be prepared to react correctly to changes in the traffic ahead.

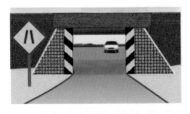

What should a driver do on the approach to this situation?
ABMW0283R

Reduce speed and stop if necessary.

When road priority is unclear you might have to yield to oncoming vehicles. Never drive a vehicle into an area that it might not be able to clear or where it could cause an obstruction or bottleneck.

When driving on this one-way street with vehicles parked on both sides, what should a driver be prepared for? ABMW0288R
Pedestrians crossing between the vehicles.

When driving on a one-way street, you should be extra careful and be prepared to react to a change in the traffic situation.

What should a driver do in this situation when intending to turn left? ABMW0290R
Wait and allow both pedestrians to cross.

By law you must yield to pedestrians already crossing at a junction. Pedestrians are vulnerable road users and you should be extra careful driving at places where pedestrians are attempting to cross the road.

What should a driver be aware of when driving at night along a shopping street with many different light sources? ABMW0294R
Traffic lights may be difficult to distinguish from the other bright lights.

When driving at night in an area where there is a variety of light sources, you need to be extra careful, as potential hazards might be more difficult to see.

The driver is approaching traffic lights that they know have been green for some time. What should the driver do? ABMW0316R
The driver should prepare to stop in case the lights change before they reach them.

You should always read the road ahead and be prepared to react to changing traffic situations. Where traffic lights have been green for some time, you should be prepared to stop, as the lights are probably about to change to amber.

What should the driver do if there are cattle on the road ahead? ABMW0318R
The driver should reduce speed and overtake with care.

You should always read the road ahead and be prepared to react to changing traffic situations. If you meet cattle or other animals on the road, you should slow down and be prepared to stop . Don't use the horn or do anything that might frighten the animals. You must stop if directed to do so by the person in charge of animals.

What should drivers be aware of if they meet horses with riders on the road? ABMW0320R
Drivers should be aware that loud noises from their vehicle may frighten the horses and cause them to bolt.

You must know your responsibilities towards animal traffic on the road. Horses are easily startled and any sudden noises or activity could cause them to bolt.

What should the driver do when approaching a humpbacked hill? ABMW0321R
The driver should reduce speed, keep to the left and be alert for hazards ahead.

As you approach a humpbacked bridge or hill, you should be aware that there might be hidden dangers ahead – for example, overtaking traffic coming towards you. You should always read the road ahead and be prepared to react to changing traffic situations such as this.

What should a driver do if there is a large oil spill on the road? ABMW0322R
Reduce speed by gently applying the brakes and switch on the hazard warning lights.

Where oil is spilt on the road, your tyres will have reduced grip, and you might be at risk of skidding if you brake sharply. If you do come across oil on the road, brake gently and switch on your hazard warning lights for a short period to alert other traffic to the hazard.

What do flashing amber beacons on an oncoming vehicle alert a driver to? ABMW0323R
That the oncoming vehicle may be slow moving or extra wide.

Flashing amber beacons are used by recovery vehicles and vehicles carrying abnormal loads. You should be aware that these vehicles may need extra room and could conceal following traffic. When you come across such vehicles, slow down and be prepared to stop if necessary.

1
2

149

What should a driver do if they meet a vehicle with flashing amber beacons?

ABMW0324R

Slow down and prepare to stop.

Flashing amber beacons are used by recovery vehicles and vehicles carrying abnormal loads. You should be aware that these vehicles may need extra room and could conceal following traffic. When you come across such vehicles, slow down and be prepared to stop if necessary.

What should a driver be aware of before crossing railway or tram lines?

There may be an uneven surface and tyre grip may be reduced when crossing the rails.

ABMW0325R

You should be aware of the impact of changes in the road surface. For example, at railway and tram crossings the uneven surface or oil deposits could reduce the grip of your tyres. Slow down as you approach railway or tram crossings and increase your distance from the vehicle in front.

What should the driver be aware of when crossing road markings such as lines and directional arrows?

The stopping distance is increased due to reduced tyre grip.

ABMW0326R

You should be aware of the impact of changes in the road surface. For example, road markings and directional arrows can become slippery when wet. Where possible, avoid driving on road markings, and be aware of the increased risk of skidding.

When should signals (for example, with indicators) be given to other road users?

ABMW0341R

Clearly and in good time to let other road users know your intentions.

Giving signals is a way of telling other road users what you intend to do. So, you should signal properly before moving off, turning right or left, changing lanes, overtaking, slowing down or stopping. Signal clearly and in good time, and keep in mind that giving a signal does not give you the right of way.

How does giving a late signal affect other road users?

ABMW0343R

They may not have sufficient time to react.

Giving signals is a way of telling other road users what you intend to do. So, you should signal properly before moving off, turning right or left, changing lanes, overtaking, slowing down or stopping. Signal clearly and in good time, and keep in mind that giving a signal does not give you the right of way. Late signals may confuse other road users.

What should a driver do if they do not want to travel as fast as the vehicle in front?

ABMW0362R

The driver should keep to the left and allow vehicles to overtake if they wish.

Always read the road ahead and be prepared to react to any traffic situation. You should not drive so slowly that your vehicle unnecessarily blocks other road users. If you want to allow a vehicle behind to overtake, you may pull into the hard shoulder briefly as long as no pedestrians or cyclists are using it and there are no junctions or entrances nearby.

What should a driver do if they wish to drive across a busy road and the traffic lights which normally control the junction are temporarily out of action?

ABMW0365R

Take good observation, wait for a clear break in the traffic and proceed to cross the road.

Always read the road ahead and be prepared to react to any traffic situation. In this case, do not proceed until it is clear and safe to do so. Do not assume that you have the right of way.

1

2

When is it permitted to force oncoming traffic onto the hard shoulder on the opposite side of the road while overtaking?

ABMW0372R

It is not permitted to force oncoming traffic onto the hard shoulder while overtaking.

Overtaking in the manner described here is dangerous. You should overtake another vehicle only when it is safe to do so, both for you and for all other traffic. Before you overtake, make sure the road ahead is clear and that you have enough room to complete the overtaking manoeuvre and return to your own side of the road without forcing any other road user to alter speed or course.

Forcing oncoming traffic onto the hard shoulder on the opposite side of the road - is this safe driving?

ABMW0373R

No, this is dangerous driving.

Overtaking in the manner described here is dangerous. You should overtake another vehicle only when it is safe to do so, both for you and for all other traffic. Before you overtake, make sure the road ahead is clear and that you have enough room to complete the overtaking manoeuvre and return to your own side of the road without forcing any other road user to alter speed or course.

When meeting oncoming traffic on a national road, is it permitted to move into the hard shoulder to allow following traffic to overtake?
Yes, temporarily when the hard shoulder is clear and it is safe to drive there while the faster traffic overtakes. ABMW0374R

On national roads, the hard shoulder is normally for the use of pedestrians and cyclists only. If you want to allow a vehicle behind to overtake, you may pull into the hard shoulder briefly as long as no pedestrians or cyclists are using it and there are no junctions or entrances nearby. In the case of motorways, however, you must not drive on the hard shoulder, except in an emergency.

When driving on a national road is it permitted to drive on the hard shoulder in order to allow faster-moving traffic to overtake?
Yes, temporarily when the hard shoulder is clear and it is safe to drive there while the traffic is overtaking. ABMW0375R

On national roads, the hard shoulder is normally for the use of pedestrians and cyclists only. If you want to allow a vehicle behind to overtake, you may pull into the hard shoulder briefly as long as no pedestrians or cyclists are using it and there are no junctions or entrances nearby. In the case of motorways, however, you must not drive on the hard shoulder, except in an emergency.

Subject to the speed limit, what is the 'safest' speed to drive at?
The speed that will enable the driver to stop the vehicle within the distance ahead that they can see to be clear. ABMW0379

You should always drive at a speed that allows you to stop within the distance ahead that you can see to be clear. If you don't think you could safely bring the vehicle to a stop within the range of what you can see, then you're driving too fast – slow down.

When stopped at traffic lights and the green light comes on, what should a driver do? ABMW0381R
Check that other road users have cleared the junction and move off with care.

When stopped at traffic lights and the green light comes on, you should check to ensure the way is clear and proceed only if it is safe to do so.

In dry weather how might a driver judge what is a safe following distance to vehicle in front? ABMW0427R
By allowing at least two seconds to elapse between the vehicle in front and the driver's own vehicle passing a fixed point.

You should maintain a gap of at least two seconds from the vehicle in front – that's the two-second rule.

1

2

What effect does towing a loaded trailer have on stopping ability?

It significantly increases stopping distance.   ABMW0434R

If you are towing a loaded trailer, you need to be aware that your braking distance could be considerably greater, depending on the weight and size of the trailer.

Is a driver allowed to sound the horn while driving in a built-up area at night?   ABMW0721R

Yes, but between 11:30pm and 7:00am the horn may be sounded only in an emergency.

You are not allowed to use the horn in a built-up area between 11:30pm and 7:00am unless there is a traffic emergency. Only use a horn to warn other road users of oncoming danger or if you need to make them aware of your presence for safety reasons. Using the horn does not give you an automatic right of way. Never use the horn to provoke a reaction from or to rebuke another motorist.

Under what circumstances is it permitted to replace the standard horn on a vehicle with a musical horn?   ABMW0722

Never.

A horn is designed to be an audible warning device. You should not make any technical modifications to the horn without professional advice as these may have legal and safety implications.

When is the use of the horn prohibited?   ABMW0723R

Between 11:30pm and 7:00am in a built-up area.

You are not allowed to use the horn in a built-up area between 11:30pm and 7:00am unless there is a traffic emergency. Only use a horn to warn other road users of oncoming danger or if you need to make them aware of your presence for safety reasons. Using the horn does not give you an automatic right of way. Never use the horn to provoke a reaction from or to rebuke another motorist.

When parked on a busy road, what should the driver be aware of?   BW0002R

Before opening the door the driver should make sure it is safe to do so.

When you park a vehicle on a busy road, make sure it is safe before opening the door, as there could be traffic passing close by.

1
2

Vulnerable Road Users

On average, how many pedestrians will be killed if hit by a car at 60 km/h? CPC1130
9 out of 10.

The link between pedestrian deaths and vehicle speed is based on research by The Royal Society for the Prevention of Accidents. Death rates may be higher where a pedestrian is hit by a large vehicle.

On average, how many pedestrians will be killed if hit by a car at 30 km/h? CPC1132
1 out of 10.

Hit by a car at 30 km per hour, one out of 10 pedestrians will be killed. Death rates may be higher where a pedestrian is hit by a large vehicle.

Which type of road users are particularly vulnerable at junctions? CD25
Cyclists.

When emerging from a junction, you should watch out for other road users such as pedestrians, who often cross at junctions. Cyclists and motorcyclists are often difficult to see at junctions and may approach faster than you think.

What road users should the driver of a large vehicle be particularly aware of on their left-hand side at traffic lights? CD26
Motorcyclists.

When at traffic lights in a large vehicle, you should watch out for vulnerable road users, such as pedestrians, cyclists and motorcyclists, who may come up on your left. Before moving off, check along the left to make sure it is safe to proceed.

There are pedestrians on the footpath ahead and there are pools of water on the road. What should a driver do? ABMW0327R
Reduce speed and try to avoid the pools of water so as not to splash the pedestrians.

During wet conditions, you should be aware that surface water can affect the stability of your vehicle. This is particularly so where the water lies in pools. As you drive through surface water, you should show consideration to pedestrians and cyclists and try not to splash them as you pass.

When a driver meets a set of traffic lights showing green and elderly pedestrians are crossing at the junction, what should the driver do?
Allow the pedestrians to cross in their own time.   CD0175R

If you are driving and meet a set of traffic lights at a junction that are showing green in your favour, but with elderly pedestrians on the crossing, you should allow the pedestrians to cross in their own time. Vehicles do not have an automatic right of way on the road and should proceed with caution at all times.

Which type of road users are particularly vulnerable at junctions?
Pedestrians.   CD0176R

When emerging from a junction, you should watch out for other road users such as pedestrians, who often cross at junctions. Cyclists and motorcyclists are often difficult to see at junctions and may approach faster than you think.

What road users should the driver of a large vehicle be particularly aware of on their left-hand side at traffic lights?   CD0177
Pedestrians.

When at traffic lights in a large vehicle, you should watch out for vulnerable road users, such as pedestrians, cyclists and motorcyclists, who may come up on your left. Before moving off, check along the left to make sure it is safe to proceed.

A driver meets a pelican crossing with a green light showing. There is a pedestrian still on the road. What should the driver do?   CD0178R
Wait patiently and let the pedestrian cross at their own pace.

If you are driving and meet a pelican crossing with the light showing green in your favour, but with a pedestrian still on the road, you should allow the pedestrian to cross in their own time. Vehicles do not have an automatic right of way on the road and should proceed with caution at all times.

When stopped at traffic lights and the green light comes on but   ABMW0528R
pedestrians are still crossing the road, what should a driver do?
Wait as long as necessary to enable them to complete the crossing.

A green traffic light means you should go if the way is clear. If pedestrians are crossing, give way to them and let them finish crossing before proceeding.

155

What way is an inexperienced learner driver likely to react in traffic situations? ABMW0532R
Slower than an experienced driver.

You should be patient when driving behind a learner driver. Learners may not anticipate and react to situations as well as an experienced driver would.

What should a driver do if the traffic light changes to green while ABMW0537R pedestrians are still crossing at traffic lights or at a pelican crossing?
Wait patiently and let them cross at ease.

You must always yield to pedestrians already crossing at a pedestrian crossing or junction, and you must not hurry them off the crossing by aggressive actions. Vehicles do not have a greater right of way over other road users.

In slow-moving city traffic, a driver should occasionally check their blind spots for which road users in particular? ABMW0539R
Cyclists.

In slow-moving city traffic, you should be aware of and check your blind spots before any manoeuvre. Cyclists can easily become 'hidden' in a blind spot, and in slow-moving traffic, they might be moving faster than you are.

What should a driver do when overtaking a cyclist? ABMW0548R
Allow extra clearance in case the cyclist swerves suddenly.

You should never cut in front of cyclists when overtaking them. Give them plenty of space especially as they may change direction suddenly – for example, to avoid a pothole, or because they are blown off course by a strong gust of wind.

What should a driver do when they see joggers ahead on the left?
Check the mirrors, indicate and overtake the joggers, allowing them sufficient clearance. ABMW0549R

People on the road are more vulnerable than vehicles so you should treat them with care. If you see people jogging ahead, use the mirror-signal-mirror (blind spots) – manoeuvre routine and give sufficient clearance to the joggers when you are overtaking them.

When driving on a road that has a potholed surface and there is a cyclist ahead, what should a driver do? ABMW0550R
Allow extra clearance in case the cyclist swerves to avoid a pothole.

You should always be aware of how vulnerable cyclists are. When you are driving on a road with potholes or bad surfaces, take into account that they may have to swerve suddenly to avoid potholes.

When driving through a residential area, what particular hazards should a driver be aware of? ABMW0554R
Children or residents may come out suddenly.

When driving through a built-up area, you should drive with care and always be ready for the unexpected – such as children running out onto the road.

When driving on a country road without footpaths, what should a driver look out for coming towards them on their side of the road? ABMW0556R
Pedestrians.

Pedestrian deaths account for one in five fatalities on our roads, so you should always be on the look-out for pedestrians, especially on country roads where there is no footpath.

What could happen if a driver parks on a footpath? ABMW0558R
Pedestrians could be impeded.

You should never park on a footpath. Pedestrians (including people with young children in pushchairs and prams) might have to go onto the road to get around your car, and this could put them in danger.

What should a driver do when driving along and there is a cyclist on the road up ahead? ABMW0559R
Check the mirrors, indicate in good time and move out if it is safe to do so.

You should overtake only when it is safe to do so. Give extra space to cyclists when you are overtaking them, as they may need to move out to avoid a pothole, or they could be blown into your path on windy days.

1
2

If indicators are not fitted or are not working, how should signals be given? ABMW0560R

By hand, clearly and in good time.

If, for whatever reason, your vehicle does not have indicators or has indicators that are not working, you should know how to use the appropriate hand signals to alert other road users of your intention to change direction.

What should a driver do when travelling on a country road with following traffic, and they meet pedestrians? ABMW0561R

Signal to following traffic their intention to overtake the pedestrians.

When you are driving on a road without footpaths, you should take extra care when you come upon pedestrians on the road. If you have to move out to overtake and there is following traffic, check your mirrors and signal in good time to alert the drivers behind that there is a hazard ahead.

In relation to cyclists, what should a driver be aware of when driving on dark winter mornings and evenings on unlit country roads? ABMW0562R

Cyclists are much more vulnerable in poor lighting conditions.

You should take extra care when driving on dark winter mornings and evenings – vulnerable road users such as cyclists and pedestrians (particularly schoolchildren) might not be so easy to see in low light conditions.

In relation to pedestrians, what should a driver be aware of when driving on dark winter mornings and evenings? ABMW0564R

That there could be vulnerable pedestrians walking in the countryside.

You should take extra care when driving on dark winter mornings and evenings – vulnerable road users such as cyclists and pedestrians (particularly schoolchildren) might not be so easy to see in low light conditions.

In relation to pedestrians, what should a driver be aware of when driving on dark winter mornings and evenings? ABMW0565R

Schoolchildren are more vulnerable on unlit country roads on dark winter mornings and evenings.

You should take extra care when driving on dark winter mornings and evenings – vulnerable road users such as cyclists and pedestrians (particularly schoolchildren) might not be so easy to see in low light conditions.

At road junctions, what type of road users are particularly vulnerable?
Pedestrians. ABMW16

Vehicles do not have an automatic right of way at junctions. As a driver you should pay particular attention to vulnerable road users such as pedestrians, cyclists and motorcyclists and be aware that they are entitled to use the road in safety.

When a driver intends to make a left-hand turn on a busy city street junction and there are pedestrians and cyclists around, what should a driver do? ABMW19
Watch for cyclists or pedestrians on the left.

The vehicle does not have a greater right-of-way than any other road user. As a driver you should pay particular attention to vulnerable road users such as pedestrians, cyclists and motorcyclists and be aware that they are entitled to use the road in safety.

In slow-moving city traffic a driver should occasionally check their blind spots for which road users in particular? ABMW22
Pedestrians.

In slow-moving city traffic, you should be aware of and check your blind spots before any manoeuvre. Pedestrians can easily become 'hidden' in a blind spot, and in slow-moving traffic, they might be moving faster than you are.

What should a driver do when driving at night on an unlit road? ABMW24
Watch out for stray animals or livestock.

While driving at night and even with the best headlights, it can be very difficult to see all the hazards that you might come across – for example, stray animals or livestock on the road. At night you should drive at a speed that will enable you to stop safely within the distance you can see to be clear ahead.

When a driver intends to make a left-hand turn on a busy city street junction and there are pedestrians and cyclists around, what should the driver do? AMBW0538R
Watch for cyclists or pedestrians who may try to cross the road in front of the vehicle.

The vehicle does not have a greater right-of-way than any other road user. As a driver you should pay particular attention to vulnerable road users such as pedestrians, cyclists and motorcyclists and be aware that they are entitled to use the road in safety.

Road Rage

To whom should a driver report aggressive driving? CPC1348
Traffic Watch.

Report all aggressive driving incidents to Traffic Watch or a Garda station. They are the best people to deal with aggressive driving.

What is road rage? CPC1350
Uncontrolled anger resulting in intimidation toward another driver.

If you display road rage, it means you have uncontrolled anger that causes you to intimidate or be violent towards another driver.

Why is tailgating (driving too close to the vehicle in front) a dangerous practice? CD1342
It can restrict the driver's view of the road ahead.

If a driver does not have a good view of the road ahead, they may not be able to see or plan for hazards which may occur. Tailgating is dangerous because it restricts the view of the road ahead.

Why is tailgating (driving too close behind the vehicle in front) dangerous? ABMW0337R
The vehicle will not have sufficient distance to stop safely in an emergency.

If you drive too close to the vehicle in front and it brakes suddenly, you will not have enough time to react. For that reason you should always keep a safe distance from the vehicle in front. One way of calculating a safe distance is the 'two-second rule': allow at least two seconds to elapse between the vehicle in front and your own vehicle passing a fixed point such as a lamp post or sign post.

Is tailgating allowed on a motorway or dual carriageway? ABMW0338R
No, because the vehicle in front may stop suddenly.

If you drive too close to the vehicle in front and it brakes suddenly, you will not have enough time to react. For that reason you should always keep a safe distance from the vehicle in front. One way of calculating a safe distance is the 'two-second rule': allow at least two seconds to elapse between the vehicle in front and your own vehicle passing a fixed point such as a lamp post or sign post.

Driver Behaviour

A driver using a mobile phone is how many times more likely to have an accident?
CPC1146

Four times.

Anything that causes you to think about something other than driving is a distraction and dangerous.

What type of driving can reduce the chance of being in a road accident?

Defensive.
CPC1185

If you drive defensively you reduce your risk of being involved in a traffic accident. This means driving with anticipation and awareness.

There are limits on using the horn in built-up areas between the hours of

11:30 pm and 7:00am.
CPC1360

Do not use a horn in built-up areas between 11:30pm and 7:00am unless there is traffic emergencies.

When joining a motorway from a slip road, what should a driver do?

Adjust speed to match that of the motorway traffic, and merge into a suitable gap.
CD0173R

When joining a motorway from a slip road, adjust your speed to that of the motorway traffic and merge into a suitable gap. This may mean slowing to allow traffic in the nearside lane to pass. You should not force them to swerve or slow down to avoid your vehicle.

A large vehicle is being driven up a steep hill and there is a 'slow lane' on the left. What should the driver do?
CD0174R

Drive in the slow lane to allow other traffic overtake.

Slow lanes (also known as crawler or climbing lanes) have been introduced on some roads to allow large slow-moving vehicles get out of the way of faster-moving traffic. When driving a large vehicle, you should use such lanes where possible to help improve traffic flow.

A truck driver is late with a delivery and there is a bus lane in operation ahead, what should a driver do? C0088R
Not drive in the bus lane.

Bus lanes are operational at the times indicated on the accompanying plate. Only buses, taxis and cyclists may drive in the bus lanes at these times.

In what circumstances may a truck driver use the hard shoulder of a motorway? C6
When stopping in an emergency or breakdown.

If, when driving on a motorway, your vehicle develops a problem, leave the motorway immediately if possible. If this is not possible, pull in and stop on the hard shoulder as far as possible to the left. Turn on your hazard lights and contact the emergency services without delay.

What should a driver do on a narrow road when another vehicle is coming in the opposite direction? ABMW0330R
Reduce speed and allow reasonable clearance between their vehicle and the oncoming one before proceeding.

You should always be prepared to react to hazards ahead. When you meet a vehicle coming against you on a narrow road, you should show consideration and slow down to a appropriate speed so that the two vehicles can pass each other safely.

When driving along and wishing to stop at a shop on the side of the street in order to make a purchase, what should a driver do? ABMW0331R
Continue on to a safe parking space.

You may park only where it is safe and legal to do so. Your parked vehicle must not cause a danger or an obstruction to other road users

When a driver is driving behind another vehicle that they do not intend to overtake, what should the driver do? ABMW0332R
Keep well back to allow following traffic to overtake them.

You should always allow sufficient distance between your vehicle and the vehicle in front. This will enable you to stop safely if necessary, and it will give overtaking vehicles enough room to pull in safely to the left lane after they have passed you.

When a driver is driving in a line of traffic and does not intend to overtake, what should the driver do?

ABMW0333R

Stay back and leave a gap for other drivers to overtake.

You should always allow sufficient distance between your vehicle and the vehicle in front. This will enable you to stop safely if necessary, and it will give overtaking vehicles enough room to pull in safely to the left lane after they have passed you.

What traffic may use a contra-flow bus lane?

ABMW0474

Buses on a scheduled service.

A bus lane is a special lane for the use of buses. Taxis and cyclists may use some bus lanes. A contra-flow bus lane is one that runs in the opposite direction to traffic beside it. Only buses on a scheduled service may use a contra-flow bus lane.

What traffic may use a with-flow bus lane during the specified times?

Buses, taxis and cyclists.

ABMW0475R

A bus lane is a special lane for the use of buses. A 'with-flow' bus lane is one that runs in the same direction as the traffic beside it. Taxis and cyclists may also use with-flow bus lanes. Other traffic may use them outside the hours posted on the accompanying plate.

When driving along a dual carriageway, what lane position should a driver be in?

ABMW0477R

In the left-hand lane unless the driver wishes to overtake or turn right.

You must normally drive in the left-hand lane of a dual carriageway, except when overtaking or turning right a short distance ahead.

What does a 2-plus-1 road have?

ABMW0480R

Two non-motorway lanes in one direction and one non-motorway lane in the opposite direction.

A 2-plus-1 road consists of two lanes in one direction of travel and one lane in the other direction. The two-lane section allows for safe overtaking and alternates with a one-lane section roughly every 2 kilometres.

On a 2-plus-1 road, where must a driver only turn right?
ABMW0481R
At controlled junctions.

A 2-plus-1 road consists of two lanes in one direction of travel and one lane in the other direction. There may be safety barriers separating the two directions of traffic, so in this situation you may turn right only at junctions.

What does a 2-plus-1 road have?
ABMW0482R
Two lanes of traffic in one direction and one in the opposite direction.

A 2-plus-1 road consists of two lanes in one direction of travel and one lane in the other direction. The two-lane section allows for safe overtaking and alternates with a one-lane section roughly every 2 kilometres.

Where may a driver overtake on a 2-plus-1 road?
ABMW0483R
In the two-lane stretch.

A 2-plus-1 road consists of two lanes in one direction of travel and one lane in the other direction. When you need to overtake, you should wait until you reach the 2-lane section which occurs approximately every 2 kilometres.

What should a driver do when travelling on a motorway or dual carriageway?
ABMW0484R
Be alert for other drivers who may suddenly change lanes or reduce speed.

Motorways and dual carriageways are designed to help traffic travel faster and more safely between destinations. Traffic conditions can change very quickly because of the speed and increased volumes of traffic and lanes, and you need to be particularly alert to other drivers changing lanes or reducing speed.

When driving on a motorway and wishing to turn back, what should a driver do?
ABMW0490R
Leave the motorway at the next exit and cross to the other side using the fly-over (or underpass).

If you miss your intended exit when driving on a motorway, you should proceed to the next junction exit where you can leave the motorway and then rejoin it in the opposite direction.

What should a driver do when leaving a motorway?

ABMW0492R

Comply with the speed limit on the road the driver is joining.

When you are leaving a motorway, enter the deceleration lane and reduce your speed. Comply with the speed limit of the road you are entering – most likely you will be in a 2-way traffic system where you will encounter vulnerable road users.

What should a driver do if they drive past their intended exit by mistake?

Drive on and leave at the next exit.

ABMW0493R

If you miss your intended exit when driving on a motorway, you should proceed to the next junction exit where you can leave the motorway and then rejoin it the opposite direction.

What should a driver do in order to keep alert during a long journey?

Increase the air circulation and make regular stops if necessary.

BW0018R

While on a long journey, you should take regular rest breaks. A short walk and a caffeinated drink (tea or coffee) can help to revive you. Keep the vehicle cool and well ventilated with a steady flow of fresh air.

What effect would exhaust gases leaking into a vehicle have on the driver?

BW0020R

The driver may become drowsy or ill.

Exhaust gases leaking into a vehicle can make the driver drowsy or ill, and this can lead to a serious collision. If you suspect that exhaust gases are leaking into the vehicle, you should have it checked by a qualified person.

1

2

Journey planning

When estimating the time for a journey, what should a driver allow extra time for? CD0034R

Driving during 'rush-hour' traffic.

A journey will nearly always take longer than expected because of traffic jams, road works, adverse weather conditions, and so on. A driver should understand this and allow sufficient time to complete the journey in a safe manner.

When estimating the time for a journey, what should a driver allow extra time for? CD0035R

Mandatory rest breaks.

A journey will nearly always take longer than expected because of traffic jams, road works, adverse weather conditions, and so on. A driver should understand this and allow sufficient time to complete the journey in a safe manner.

A driver comes to a bridge with a weight limit that is lower than their vehicle's weight. What should the driver do? CD0038

Turn around and find an alternative route.

A driver should know the weight of their vehicle, and if they encounter a regulatory sign indicating a weight limit that is lower than their vehicle's weight, they must not proceed past the sign. They should take an alternative route.

When estimating the time for a journey, what should a driver allow extra time for? CD2

Stoppages due to road works.

A journey will nearly always take longer than expected because of traffic jams, road works, adverse weather conditions, and so on. A driver should understand this and allow sufficient time to complete the journey in a safe manner.

When estimating the time for a journey, what should a driver allow extra time for?
CD3

Driving during adverse weather conditions.

A journey will nearly always take longer than expected because of traffic jams, road works, adverse weather conditions, and so on. A driver should understand this and allow sufficient time to complete the journey in a safe manner.

When estimating the time for a journey, what should a driver allow extra time for?
CD4

Minor repairs to the vehicle.

A journey will nearly always take longer than expected because of traffic jams, road works, adverse weather conditions, and so on. A driver should understand this and allow sufficient time to complete the journey in a safe manner.

1

2

When estimating the time for a journey, what should a driver allow extra time for?
CD5

Delays due to traffic incidents.

A journey will nearly always take longer than expected because of traffic jams, road works, adverse weather conditions, and so on. A driver should understand this and allow sufficient time to complete the journey in a safe manner.

General

Industry regulation

Who regulates the truck and bus industries in Ireland?   CPC1376
Department of Transport.

The Department of Transport is the regulator for both passenger and road haulage operations.

Who enforces the licensing provisions of the Road Transport Acts?   CD1349
The Road Safety Authority and An Garda Síochána.

The Road Safety Authority is responsible for enforcing the licencing provisions of the Road Transport Acts.

Road Haulage and Road Passenger Transport Operator's Licenses are issued and maintained by   CD1350
The Department of Transport.

The Department of Transport is the regulator for both passenger and road haulage operations.

Which of the following organisations is responsible for enforcing EU and national transport legislation on the licensing of road haulage and passenger operators?   CD1351
The Road Safety Authority.

The Road Safety Authority is the regulator for both passenger and road haulage operations.

Which of the following operators requires a Road Haulage Operator's Licence? C1314

An operator that is transporting a customer's goods for hire.

A Road Haulage Operator's Licence is required to carry goods for hire or reward in a vehicle or combination of vehicles that has a maximum authorised mass greater than 3.5 tonnes.

Which of the following operators requires a Road Passenger Transport Operator's Licence? D1306

An operator that is carrying 9 or more passengers for hire in a vehicle constructed to do so.

A Road Passenger Transport Operator's Licence is required to carry passengers by road for hire or reward in vehicles constructed and equipped to carrying nine or more passengers.

Customer Disputes

If involved in a dispute with an angry person who threatens the company with legal action, the driver should CPC1379

remain calm and in control of the situation.

As you represent the company, you must behave in a professional way. The company's reputation and, to some extent, liability depend on you.

When a driver is involved in a dispute while on duty, the company may suffer commercially and financially because CPC1382

the driver is a representative of the company.

As you represent the company, you must behave in a professional way. The company's reputation and, to some extent, liability depend on you.

Dealing with customers with disabilities

When dealing with a passenger with a visual impairment a driver should
tell them if there is anything blocking their way as they get on or off the
bus.   D1307

Alerting a passenger with a visual impairment to the presence of any obstacles in their path
helps ensure they get on or off the bus safely.

**When dealing with a passenger who is deaf or hard of hearing a driver
should**   D1308
Speak clearly and at normal speed.

Speaking clearly and at normal speed helps a passenger who is lip reading to understand.

**When dealing with a passenger with a physical disability, such as
arthritis or multiple sclerosis, a driver should**   D1309
give them time to get to their seats before moving off.

Giving a passenger with a physical disability time to get to their seat before moving off
helps to ensure that they have a safe and comfortable journey.

**A wheelchair user boards the vehicle and wishes to use the docking area,
which is occupied with standing passengers and their baggage. What
should the driver do?**   D1311
Ask the passengers to move.

A wheelchair user seated in his/her wheelchair must only be carried in a docking area.
Drivers must ensure that the passenger can get in to and out of the docking area and
that it is free for their use.

**To safely deploy a lift or ramp for use by a wheelchair user a driver
should**   D1312
Position the vehicle as close as possible to the kerb.

Positioning the vehicle as close as possible to the kerb allows the ramp or lift to be
deployed onto the pavement, helping a wheelchair user to safely and comfortably get on
or off the bus.

In which of the following locations may a wheelchair user be carried in a bus or coach?   D1313
In the docking area.

A wheelchair user seated in his/her wheelchair must only be carried in a docking area.

A dog which is used by a child with autism is a   D1314
assistance dog.

Assistance dogs are trained to undertake practical tasks to support a person with a disability. An assistance dog for a child with autism acts as a calming focus, enabling a child to remain safe and feel secure in places the child may find challenging.

A driver's responsibility with regard to a wheelchair restraint system is to   D1315
ensure that the passenger is secured with the appropriate seat belt.

To ensure a safe journey, it is of the utmost importance that the wheelchair user is secured in the wheelchair with the appropriate vehicle seatbelt.

What should a bus driver do when communicating with a passenger who is hard of hearing?   RSA01023
Driver should look at the passenger when speaking to them.

As a professional bus driver you should be aware of how to communicate with passengers who have special needs. When communicating with a passenger who is hard of hearing you should look at them when speaking to them, this allows for facial expressions to be understood.

What should a driver do when a deaf person gets on the bus?   RSA01028
Look at the passenger when speaking to them.

Drivers must be sympathetic towards passengers who have special needs and treat them fairly.

Case Studies
Trucks

Case Study No.1

Gavin drove a refrigerated truck for Pugh's Produce. He was responsible for delivering fresh produce to supermarkets around Ireland. This morning, Gavin's job was to drive from Dublin to Cork with a large truck full of crates of lettuce. He had a scheduled "delivery window" of noon to 1:00 pm. After loading the crates into the truck and stacking them evenly and at a low level, Gavin calculated the weight of the truck with the crates. He was satisfied that the weight was under the maximum permitted axle weight and gross vehicle weight (GVW).

Gavin performed the daily walk-around and cockpit checks of his vehicle. He checked the following:

Gavin found everything to be in order after he completed his checks. As he inserted his tachograph chart, he remembered that he needed to get another tachograph calibration certificate as his was issued seven years ago. He was not going to do that today. He hoped that he would not have to provide his certificate for inspection on this delivery.

Gavin's Walk-Around Check
Brakes
Lights & Indicators
Tyres & Wheel Securing
 Nuts and Markers
Mirrors/Glass
Speedometer
Tachograph
Number Plates
Reflectors
Exhaust System
Correct plating
Current Test Certificate
Insurance
Seat Belts
Load Being Carried

Gavin's Cockpit Drill
Doors
Seat
Handbrake
Mirrors
Fuel

Gavin began his journey mid-morning feeling relaxed, refreshed, and fully alert. From his years as a professional truck driver, he had learned to get adequate rest before a long drive. His delivery destination in Cork was about 250 kilometres away. Gavin knew that his progress would be delayed because the number of trucks on the roads had increased in recent years. Taking into account unloading time, he hoped to reach home by mid-afternoon.

On this trip Gavin would have to travel on his least favourite route, which was a long stretch of a single lane road. While on the road, he came upon a car going significantly under the speed limit. Since the car was travelling slowly and the oncoming lane was clear, Gavin decided to pass the vehicle. He signalled, overtook the car, quickly switched back into the correct lane, and checked his mirrors. However, he did not immediately see the car in his mirrors when he switched back into the correct lane.

At one point during the trip, Gavin was not paying close attention to the road and suddenly realised that he had to make a quick left turn to keep on his route. He hit the brakes but still took the corner very fast. The pressure of the turn caused the trailer door to open. Some of the heads of lettuce rolled out onto the road, indicating that one of the crates had opened and spilled due to an obviously unsecured door. Gavin knew he had to pull over and assess the situation. Not seeing any "No Parking" signs, he parked on the left side of the road, parallel with the kerb. Since the ground was level, he put the transmission into neutral, got out of the cab, and headed to the back of the truck to assess the situation. As he secured the cargo and door, he remembered that he had not checked the rear doors before starting his journey.

Fortunately, there were no other vehicles following him when he had turned left. Gavin was able to collect the lettuce that had spilled onto the road. He decided he would dispose of it at his next stop. He was grateful that he was not responsible for the lettuce that had been damaged.

As Gavin drove into Cork, the traffic was heavy and it was raining hard. He kept the same separation distance from the car ahead of him as he had before it began raining. He was thankful that he had made good time before the rain started. He knew he was well within the scheduled delivery window. It looked like he would get home in the afternoon as he had planned. Gavin arrived at the supermarket at 12:30 pm.

1

2

Case Study No.2

Jim drove heavy vehicles and tankers for the past 10 years and was qualified for International Carriage of Dangerous Goods by Road (ADR) Class 3 goods for the past seven years. This morning, Jim's job was to take an empty tanker to a fuel distribution depot. He collected his documentation from the traffic clerk and made sure he was carrying his ADR authorisation and driver's digital tachograph card. He downloaded the card only five days ago (his truck was fitted with a digital tachograph). Jim needed both documents today because of the type of work he was doing.

After completing his vehicle checks and "nil defect" report form, Jim checked all the safety equipment to make sure it complied with his ADR authorisation. He drove to the fuel depot with the empty tanker. The tanker was a rigid four-axle, fitted with single wheels providing extended tracking width. It had road-friendly suspension, a design gross vehicle weight (DGVW) of 32,000 kilograms, was 3.7 metres high, and had the most up-to-date tanker specifications and fuel compartments.

Jim arrived at the fuel distribution depot and complied with all the site and safety regulations pointed out by the depot supervisor. He noticed the familiar difference in how the truck handled with the full load of liquid, especially if he relaxed the footbrake when stopping. Today, Jim was to deliver a load of diesel to a large haulage yard. He had delivered to this yard before so he was able to carefully plan his route. The direct route to the haulage yard had a bridge with a weight restriction of 20,000 kilograms. There was also a low bridge just before the haulage yard.

On his way, Jim came across a road block with a detour sign that directed him onto an unfamiliar road. He knew the detour would add time to his route so he picked up speed. While driving around a sharp right-hand bend in the road he hit the brakes lightly. When he felt the wheels begin to lift slightly, he took his foot off the accelerator and drove to the outside of the bend. He then felt the wheels firmly on the road again. However, his relief was short-lived.

Continuing on, Jim arrived at the foot of a long, steep incline. Halfway up the hill he noticed a sign at a junction which indicated that no large goods vehicles (LGVs) with three or more axles were allowed. He knew that the detour route would be the shortest way back to his planned route so he decided to ignore the sign. Soon enough, he joined up with his planned route.

When Jim arrived at the haulage operator's yard he braked to a stop. Just before he came to a final halt, he relaxed the brakes and felt a sudden force acting on his truck.

The operator asked him to dispense half the load at the site and deliver the other half to a different site. Jim agreed and carefully dispensed the fuel evenly from the correct compartments. However, he failed to notice an initial spillage. He then drove to his final drop-off point and unloaded the remaining fuel.

1

2

Case Study No.3

Graham was an owner-operator who lived in Dublin and typically hauled a variety of goods. On this trip, he planned to deliver pallets of various products. The estimated road time for the journey would be three days. Graham had just taken his weekly rest of 45 hours and planned to head out early Monday morning. He wanted to make good time so that he could eat dinner at a reasonable hour, enjoy a restful night's sleep, and get another early start on Tuesday.

Graham was driving a three-axle truck with road-friendly suspension and a design gross vehicle weight (DGVW) of 24 tonnes. He checked the plate and calculated the weight to make sure his vehicle was not overloaded. This was a real concern to Graham as he had broken this rule on his last trip. To make matters worse, he was also involved in a minor accident on that trip. Even though Graham did not damage the front of his cab or the back of the truck that he hit, he reported the accident to his insurance company, just to be on the safe side. Graham and his insurance agent then realised that, during that trip, his load had exceeded the legal weight. He remembered the stress the situation had caused him. He did not want to go through that worry again.

Since Graham would be hauling to Spain and his combined weight with the load would be about 24 tonnes, he checked all of his paperwork. He made sure that he had the proper licence, consignment note, and other required documentation with him in his truck. He also remembered to double-check the issue date of his National Road Haulage Operator's Licence as he knew it would be expiring the following month. Graham confirmed that all his papers were in order. He then went through each item on his systems checklist and verified that everything on the list was in working order.

Graham loaded the 22 Euro pallet for delivery and double-checked that the pallets had not shifted. He also checked that the lashings were in good condition and attached at the proper anchorage points even though he knew he would be checking them again after a few kilometres. One of the pallet lashings had been shortened due to previous damage so Graham attached it to a strap holding the cargo to a pallet. Finally, he covered the cargo with load sheets, attached the webbing straps, and did a check of the sheeting and roping before tucking a loose rope end next to a rear light under the sheet.

Graham was on the road at 7:00 am on Monday morning. By noon, he was hungry and stopped to eat a quick lunch. After finishing and paying for his meal, he

Graham's Walk-Around Check
Brakes
Lights & Indicators
Tyres & Nuts/Markers
Horn
Mirrors
Windscreen Wipers
Tachograph
Speedometer
Exhaust System
Correct Plating

climbed into the truck cab for the last leg of that day's trip. He checked his watch and noticed it was 1:00 pm. He wanted to make good time and realised that to get to his planned destination by 5:00 pm, he would need to go just slightly over the posted speed limit.

It was raining quite heavily as Graham drove through northern France but he was confident that even with the weight of his load, he would still be able to brake and stop properly if he had to make an emergency stop. However, Graham was affected by the glare from the lights of oncoming vehicles. He switched off his headlights and pulled closer to the car in front of him but maintained a two-second gap.

After a long day on the road, Graham finally pulled into the rest area at 6:00 pm. He wanted to get another early start the next day so he took a reduced daily rest period. He hoped to get through customs by 9:00 am and would need to get his papers in order before getting on the road in the morning. As he settled in for the evening and ran through the next day's schedule, he realised that he might have to cross some bridges in the region. He would have to check the truck height in the morning and review the details of his route. Graham had recently seen a photograph in the newspaper showing the damage to a trailer caused by going under a low bridge. He wanted to make sure he did not repeat that truck driver's mistake. The newspaper photo was vivid in his mind and was the last thing he thought about as he drifted off to sleep.

Case Study No.4

Peter was an experienced heavy goods vehicle (HGV) driver. On his next trip, he was to deliver dangerous goods, both nationally and internationally. Peter held the required training certificate and had three years left on his International Carriage of Dangerous Goods by Road (ADR) licence. He also held Certificates of Professional Competence (CPCs) in goods and passenger vehicles and drove both types of vehicle for a living.

Before arriving for work today, Peter completed a reduced weekly rest period. At the depot, he checked out his truck which had two axles and a covered box body. When empty, the truck weighed eight tonnes. Peter performed his walk-around check and cockpit drill.

Peter was asked to drive the pre-loaded truck of packages and containers to a chemical manufacturing plant on an industrial estate about 25 kilometres away. The customer disclosed the dangerous goods and Peter agreed to carry them. He looked at the pre-loaded packages of corrosive chemicals and found that they were labelled correctly. After the delivery, Peter would bring back a tanker loaded with flammable liquid for onward transportation to France. This would be his next job.

Peter's Transport Emergency Card (Tremcard) contained the following information:

- details of the cargo,
- basic personal protection to be used, and
- the immediate action to be taken by the driver if there was a crash.

Peter made sure that his truck complied with the regulations for transporting each type of goods. He also checked that the Kemler plate was displayed and that the international consignment note was in the truck.

Peter arrived safely at his destination and parked in a supervised area. He was given a tanker to take back with him. He checked the new vehicle for roadworthiness and found it to be fine. He also noticed that it only had two axles (a tandem axle). At the weighbridge, the yard supervisor weighed the tanker and gave Peter a receipt. This showed that Peter was up to the weight limit with this truck. Peter was aware that the load was an international consignment.

The tanker had special plates and markings to clearly identify the contents. Peter checked that the correct symbol (based on the classification of the hazardous goods) could be seen on the tanker.

As he drove along the motorway, Peter skipped some of the intermediate gears. It had started to rain slightly. He felt a little drowsy and decided to listen to the radio. As he searched for a good radio station, he did not notice that there was a crash ahead. Suddenly, he heard a loud screech and looked up. Unfortunately, it was too late. Peter slammed on the brakes, lost control, and the tanker rolled over. Flammable liquids began to leak from the tanker.

Witnesses at the crash scene immediately called the fire and rescue services. Peter told them not to use their mobile phones so close to the tanker. The fire and rescue service arrived quickly before the tanker and liquids had a chance to catch fire. Peter told them about the tanker's contents and led the onlookers to safety. Soon a crane arrived to help get the tanker upright. Gardaí diverted traffic and the fire and rescue service cleaned up the spill. Luckily, no one was injured, including Peter.

Peter would not be able to deliver the liquid goods to France. He was worried about the conversation he was going to have with the sender. When he arrived back at his base, he told his boss that he would need a signed and witnessed letter giving details of his rest days during the previous three weeks. He had his digital tachograph card and analogue charts for the last 21 days. Peter finished work, went home, and took a regular weekly rest period. He would contact the sender of the liquid goods in the morning.

Case Study No.5

Larry operated his own haulage business in Ireland and was a regular driver of "low loader" trucks. His job this morning was to collect a new excavator from the Dublin docks and deliver it to a customer in Kerry. When he arrived at work, he changed into his overalls and work boots with protective toe caps. He collected his bag from the locker. This contained Larry's high-visibility wear, work gloves, pencil, pens, clipboard, camera, and first aid kit. Larry then collected his documents and instructions for the journey from the clerk in the office.

Larry checked the address and his road map. In planning his route, he considered the truck's height, weight, and physical restrictions. For this journey, he would be driving a one-year-old truck fitted with the original digital tachograph. After reading his documents, he realised that he would be delivering a heavy, wide excavator to a quarry.

Larry found his vehicle in the depot. He noticed that it was a beaver-tail low loader with four axles. He did his walk-around check and then completed his company's "nil defect" report sheet. He attached this to his clipboard with the other documentation his supervisor had given him. He climbed up into his cab and placed his clipboard inside the glove compartment and asked his helper to get into the truck. He then carried out his cockpit drill. Shortly after moving off, he realised that he had not turned off his mobile phone.

Larry's Cockpit Drill
Gauges working
Documentation
Sufficient fuel
Wheels unchalked
Gear selector
Mirrors
Reflectorised side markings
Map holder

Larry's Walk-Around Check
Brakes
Lights & Indicators
Radio System
Tyres & Nuts/Markers
Horn
Mirrors
Windscreen Wipers & Washers
Vehicle History
Tachograph
Speedometer
Exhaust System
Number Plates

When Larry arrived at the docks he opened the door fully and, facing the cab, climbed down using the steps and grab handles. He then contacted the freight manager, who located the excavator. The manager told him to put on his safety jacket and then load his truck. Larry did as he was asked. The excavator started easily and Larry drove it slowly onto the truck. Once in position, he parked the excavator safely then lowered the machine bucket onto the floor of the truck. He had to use the outriggers on the truck when loading the machine, as the excavator was a little wider than the floor of the truck. Larry then attached restraints onto the lashing points on the truck. Since it was a wide load, he used warning markers fitted with lights, as the day was overcast and it might be dark before he reached his destination. When he was finished, he checked the lights and switched on the amber beacon bar on the cab and a warning beacon on the truck to alert other road users of the wide load. Before leaving the port, Larry completed the consignment note and made sure to keep the correct copy for himself.

Larry's route was along the N7 dual carriageway. While signalling left and slowing to make a tight left turn into St. Margaret's Road, which leads to the N7, Larry noticed a cyclist in his left mirror. The cyclist was beginning to move up the left side (nearside) of the truck. Larry continued to watch his left mirror. He muttered to himself, recalling how the previous day he had encountered a cyclist wearing reflective clothing, riding on the left in the city centre. Larry noticed the cyclist glancing over his right shoulder. Larry heard a horn blow and saw a car approaching on his right side. The car was warning Larry that the rear overhang of the truck had swung into the bicycle's path.

Larry was agitated by these events and, once around the corner, he tried to make up some time. He approached the next right-hand corner a little fast, braking on the corner. He had to steer hard to avoid hitting the kerb.

Once on the dual carriageway the drive went smoothly until the left front of the truck began to shake wildly and the steering wheel began to vibrate. Before Larry could say "blow-out," his tyre burst. Holding the steering wheel firmly, he carefully crossed onto the hard shoulder. A chunk of rubber slapped about inside the wheel arch as Larry brought the truck to a gentle stop. When the lorry was completely stopped, Larry put on his high-visibility vest and told his helper to remain seated while he got off to check the situation. He displayed his warning triangle and tried to stop traffic by waving his arms. When he was unable to stop traffic, he got back into the truck and turned on his hazard warning lights. He then contacted the depot and a repair truck soon arrived to fix the puncture. When the repair had been completed, Larry quickly checked his load.

As he got close to Kerry, he had to slam on his breaks to avoid hitting some sheep that were crossing the road. The excavator rolled towards the cab. Luckily, there were no other vehicles around. He attached extra restraints to secure the excavator. He made it to Kerry within his time window, which was a half-hour short of the industry standard.

1

2

Case Study No.6

Robert had a national Road Haulage Operator's Licence and operated within Ireland. He usually carried ceramics, fine glassware, and collectibles, but he also had another truck that he used to carry pigs for local neighbours. Robert was paid cash for carrying his customers' goods.

On today's trip, Robert would be carrying fragile goods. While the packages were being loaded onto pallets and into the truck, Robert checked the quantity, the overall condition of the goods, and the packaging. The fragile goods were packed in appropriate containers labelled "Fragile – Handle with Care". This was a light load and Robert was not sure how to secure it.

The sender and Robert completed a consignment note and the sender kept the correct copy. The customer had chosen Robert to carry the goods because he offered "company's risk" contracts. She also had confidence in road freight and did not want the fragile goods sitting on the railway tracks for a long time.

Once he had secured the load, Robert did his routine walk-around check and cockpit drill to make sure everything was in order.

He set off at 9:15 pm. After driving for four hours, Robert decided to pull into a service area. He parked in the truck parking area and switched off the engine and rested for 45 minutes. Before driving on Robert wanted to make sure the containers were still intact from the journey so far. As he checked the load, he noticed that there were broken strands on some of the ropes. His delivery

Robert's Cockpit Drill
Documentation
Parking Brake
Side Markings
Map Holder
Warning Systems
Gear Selector
Interior Mirrors

Robert's Walk-Around Check
Brakes
Lights & Indicators
Tyres & Nuts/Markers
Horn
Windscreen Wipers & Washers
Tachograph
Speedometer
Exhaust System
Correct Plating
Seat Belts
Reflectors

window was 6:00 am to 8:00 am so he had no time to spare. As his destination was not much further, Robert decided to continue using the same ropes and to discard them after unloading the goods. He arrived at his destination at 8:00 am. When Robert arrived at the Glimmer, Sparkle, and Shine shop, he opened the trailer to check the load and ropes before the customer came out to inspect the goods. He felt guilty about not using new ropes. Fortunately, everything looked as it did when it was loaded the day before. The customer inspected all the boxes and took delivery of the goods. Robert then discarded the frayed ropes.

In preparation for his return journey, Robert checked the truck's tyres, battery, windscreen wipers, mirrors, and brake hoses. He planned his route to avoid traffic congestion. After driving for 15 minutes, he noticed an arch bridge ahead. The headroom under the bridge was 3.9 metres (13 feet) and his truck was 3 metres (10 feet) high so he knew it would fit within the bridge restrictions. As Robert drove under the bridge, he glanced down to change the radio station and, as a result, lightly scraped the left side of the bridge. He did not think there was any damage to the trailer or the bridge. As there were no witnesses, he did not stop or report the incident to the Gardaí.

As he drove, Robert daydreamed about how fortunate he was to be driving road freight and not handling rail freight. Some of his friends who handled rail freight had lost their jobs. Although Robert was regularly away from home for days at a time, he was happy to be a truck driver.

1

2

Case Study No.7

Brenda was aware she had a very long journey from her home town of Buncrana Co. Donegal down to Limerick. She went to the staff canteen and ate a good breakfast, one which would help her concentrate on her driving over the long distance without getting hungry. Brenda's consignment included bricks, bags of cement, and boxes of insulation products. She picked up her keys from the transport manager and, before having her truck loaded, carried out her daily walk-around check and a cockpit drill.

Before helping the fork truck driver to load the truck she set her tachograph to the correct mode. In order to make the loading easier she used a sack barrow to carry the bags of cement. The bricks were distributed throughout the center of the truck. Next, the cement bags were loaded at 90-degree angles. Finally, the insulation boxes were placed around the heavier items. As she had no straps to stop the load from moving, Brenda placed the

Brenda's Walk-Around Check
Windscreen
Wipers
Windscreen
Washers
Legal Discs
Wheel Condition
Tyres
Fuel Filler Cap

Brenda's Cockpit Drill
Doors Secured
Seat Adjustment
Gear Level in Neutral
Mirrors Set
Fuel Level

tarpaulins on the load, starting from the front and moving towards the back of the truck. She used rope to secure the tarpaulins in place.

Brenda started out early to get to Limerick before lunchtime (where she wanted to take her first break). As usual, she used the National roads as much as possible, watching for traffic signs that indicated things such as danger or speed limits.

Whilst driving through Donegal she encountered numerous uphill and downhill grades, and repeatedly had to change gears. The difficult driving conditions and excessive gear changing caused her to get extremely tired, but in order to make her delivery window in Limerick she kept driving. When leaving Crusheen (a town on her route), she passed under an arch bridge with vehicle restrictions.

At one point along the N 18, she came across a slow moving motorcyclist. She tried to maintain an appropriate speed and distance, but the rider was going much too slowly. If Brenda continued at that speed, her delivery time would be deleyed. As the right lane of the dual carriageway was closed for roadwork, she decided to move closer and flash her headlights at the rider, hoping he would pull over into the hard shoulder and let her pass. A Traffic Corps Garda saw what happened and pulled Brenda over to ask her about the incident.

The Garda was aware that some of the drivers who worked for the same company as Brenda had a reputation of tampering with their tachographs. In fact, in a recent news report, he heard that one of these drivers was convicted of "altering with intent to deceive" and received the maximum penalty. The Garda decided to check Brenda's tachograph. He asked her to open the tachograph and remove the chart. He then proceeded to inspect the traces made on it before handing it back to her. The tachograph was all in order, and she had the previous 21 days charts with her. However, he did not ask to see them.

As anticipated, Brenda arrived late to her destination, where she was asked to provide the transport contract documents to the authorised person. The supervisor agreed to unload the truck and, as that gave Brenda an hour and a half, she decided to go off and enjoy her evening meal. She returned at 7:00 pm at which time the staff and the supervisor left, forcing Brenda to finish unloading the last few bags of cement.

At 7:45 pm, when the unloading was complete, Brenda began the return journey which was to take her 6 and a ½ hours. After driving for only 3 kilometers Brenda remembered that she had forgot to change the mode switch on the tachograph to the correct position. She knew that it recorded the speed, distance, and time travelled. Whilst driving and correcting the mode switch setting, she decided to check the chart to make sure it was still recording. Brenda did this by opening the tachograph head whilst driving along the straight stretch of road.

Whilst passing through Oranmore she realized she had not had the consignment note signed. Deciding it was too late to do anything about it now, she kept driving on. Because this had been a long day, she was now feeling very tired. In order to get home as soon as possible she kept driving and arrived back at her depot at 3:30 am.

Case Study No.8

Today, Lorraine was going to drive her three axle, rigid truck fitted with a freezer full of containers of potato scone dough from Dublin to Barcelona. She looked forward to this journey because she had just finished two weeks holiday at home.

Lorraine knew this was an international journey, so she brought her previous tachograph charts for the days she had worked. She was also given a letter of attestation by her employer. She had all the vehicle documentation including the correct operator's licence that she had got four years ago and a European Insurance Accident Report Form. While she was on holiday her truck was serviced, so she did not check her vehicle before using it, since the mechanic should have checked it. She did check the freezer though, because she had been caught before with a faulty freezer, and all of the frozen goods had to be thrown away.

Lorraine's customer was Sorcha's Scones, a well-known distributor of frozen potato scone dough to local markets. Her journey was taking her to Bice's, a small bakery in Barcelona. The loading bay staff took special precautions while loading Lorraine's truck. The potato dough was in containers, stacked on wooden pallets and wrapped in sheeting. Then they strapped the containers to the pallets and secured the pallets to the truck. The loaders parked the truck in the yard and joined it to an electrical connection to keep the freezer at the correct temperature.

After collecting the truck from the yard, Lorraine drove to Dublin Port, boarded the ferry, and used a driver bunk and meal voucher. The ferry arrived in Holyhead. Lorraine knew she had no time to waste in getting to Dover to catch another ferry to Calais. Her truck was one of the first off the ferry. She drove through the customs without delay and onto a clear road. Her journey to Dover began at 10:30 am and took her along the A5 leading to the M6. She had heard from other drivers on the ferry that there were roadworks.

While travelling through the contraflow roadworks on the M6, a traffic patrol car pulled Lorraine over and a police officer asked if she was aware that her rear light cluster was not working properly. When indicating her brake light flashed, and when she used her foot brake one indicator and fog light lit up. The police officer also noticed that the fuel filler cap was missing and the vehicle plate was not attached to the vehicle. Rather, the plate had been stored loosely in the passenger door pocket. So the police officer gave a vehicle probation notice to Lorraine.

Fortunately, the officer allowed her to drive away in the truck, because she was running late for Dover. However, she would not drive over the speed limit, as there were several enforcement cameras on the M25 which had a goods vehicle speed limit of 60 mph (96 km/h).

After driving for ten minutes, a bird dropped down into traffic in front of Lorraine's truck. She braked and swerved to avoid hitting it. The truck almost tipped over, but Lorraine's quick thinking and driving experience kept the truck on all of its tyres. Once back on the roadway, she noticed that the truck was slightly slanted to the right. When she pulled over to the side of the road, she discovered that the right front tyre was flat. She phoned her depot who arranged a company to replace the tyre and with the help of a professional tyre fitter she got back onto the roadway.

Lorraine finally arrived in Dover at 7:15 pm, after driving the 610 km from Holyhead, and caught a ferry to Calais. Once in France, she drove on to Troyes, a journey lasting almost four hours. Following her minimum rest period she drove 1,000 km to Barcelona without stopping. When she arrived at the bakery, she parked the truck and went to her hotel for a well-deserved daily rest period.

The next day at the bakery, it took eight hours to unload the truck because there was no forklift. On the return journey, Lorraine was feeling tired and took a short nap after 800 km. She caught the ferry to Dover and during the crossing she realised she had broken the tachograph rules. She took an old chart and changed the date to suit this journey.

Eventually she got off the ferry and drove down a long steep hill to join the motorway for Holyhead. She had a three-hour delay at Holyhead before the ferry left for Dublin. Once on board the Dublin ferry she replaced the real tachograph disc with the false one. After leaving Dublin port, she met a multi-agency roadside check. An RSA Transport Officer checked her tachograph chart and noticed it had been changed. It was a very stressful day for Lorraine.

1

2

Case Study No.9

Liam was an experienced driver with over 40 years experience working in national and international road haulage carrying various loads and general haulage goods for a Dublin haulage operator. This morning he had to collect a full load of steel girders from a steelyard that was 10 km from his depot in Dublin and take the load to a construction site about 60 km in Arklow.

Liam walked out into the yard to his truck. He was the only driver of the truck, which he checked out as part of the company's defect reporting system. He found everything was okay. After doing his safety checks, he checked the equipment he needed for loading and securing the steel girders:

- a storage box containing chains,
- slings,
- securing clamps,
- lashing clamps,
- webbing straps, and
- nylon rope.

All the equipment was there and the insurance company had inspected, tested, and passed them as serviceable only two weeks ago. He also had a Certificate of Roadworthiness that was two months old.

His truck was fitted with a hydraulic on-board crane and stabilisers rated with a lifting capacity of one tonne. The crane was recently tested and certified, but Liam checked it anyway. He called back into the traffic office and collected his documentation for the journey. The load was the maximum weight he could carry as his truck was 32 tonne GVW (gross vehicle weight).

He arrived at the steelyard, spoke to the yard foreman, put on his steel-toe-capped boots, and moved his truck to where it could be loaded. The yard foreman said the forklift driver would help him in loading. While Liam was chocking his drive axle wheels on both sides of the truck, the forklift driver asked him what he wanted loaded first. Liam calculated the weight of the girders; they were various sizes ranging from 500 kg to 1500 kg. He wanted the load distributed evenly over all axles.

The truck was fitted with road-friendly air suspension. Liam was told that he did not need any special handling equipment to load the girders. He checked that he had put on the vehicle handbrake and he then stayed outside the cab while his trailer was being loaded. While loading the steel girders, one of the 1500 kg girders was damaged when the forklift operator accidentally dropped it. He told Liam about the damage and said that he was not going to load the girder on the truck. Liam agreed not to load the damaged girder.

About 30 km down the road, Liam remembered how difficult the same job was years ago when he had an old Foden truck and trailer with steel spring suspension, crossply tyres, a Fuller 9-speed "crash" gearbox, and all round drum brakes. He was enjoying how much more comfortable his current truck was and was very relaxed listening to a CD. All of the sudden, a car honked steadily at Liam, and he noticed that he had drifted into the right lane and almost hit the other vehicle. He corrected his driving, adjusted his seat, and turned off his CD.

After the incident, Liam was pulled over by Garda and they asked him for his documentation. After he gave the Garda the correct set of documents, the Garda reviewed the documentation and visually checked the truck. When the Garda found no defects, the officer demanded that Liam do a breath test. Once the officer found that there were no offences, he sent Liam on his way without further action.

After arriving at the building site, Liam made sure the ground underneath was stable and strong enough to hold the weight before unloading his truck. He stopped, put on the parking brake, and began unloading the steel. Just before he left, he phoned his boss who asked him to put the truck in the secure compound where it was that morning.

The next day Liam returned to the depot for his next job, which was a truck loaded with cartons of silk cloth. He departed at 9:00 am. He was going to drive 185 km to Galway, then changing trucks and returning with a refrigerated load of salmon caught in the Atlantic Ocean. He was going to bring it about 105 km to Tullamore before driving the remaining 80 km to his Dublin base for a very late lunch break. It would be another long day.

1

2

Case Studies
Buses

Case Study No.1

Before setting off on his day's work, John quickly checked the lights, tyres (including tyre pressures), wipers, and his emergency engine stop. At his first stop he recognised a passenger boarding the bus whom he suspected might be hard of hearing. The previous day she had asked how much the fare would be. John answered, "€1.05," while looking at someone at the back of the bus. The passenger then handed him €5 and took a seat without asking for change. At the time John wondered if she had heard him. This time, when she asked for the fare, he looked her in the eye and said, "€1.05." She smiled and gave him exactly €1.05.

As John pulled into the next stop, he noticed a passenger in a wheelchair and a woman with children. He pulled the bus close to the kerb, stopped, switched off the engine, and left the bus in first gear for safety. He lowered the bus using the kneel facility and also lowered the ramp. The woman and children boarded the bus and sat in the priority seating. John helped the passenger in the wheelchair to the docking area where some passengers were stood; he then lifted one wheel over some debris left by the passengers and applied the wheelchair brake. He drove off smoothly.

The next stop was at the new supermarket which John knew would have more passengers than any of his other stops. The bus was nearly three-quarters full with 35 passengers. John quickly calculated how many more passengers with heavy packages he could take. When he arrived at the supermarket he was relieved to find fewer passengers than he'd anticipated. However, the bus was near capacity, a fact proven by the effort needed to move off.

John pulled away, shifting gears quickly to keep the revs low. His bus was an older model but the company had an excellent maintenance schedule. Also, John usually did small checks of his own such as regularly checking tyre pressures, lights, and the emergency engine stop. After John moved off, he travelled along the road in the opposite direction to the rest of the traffic. However, he approached a right-hand corner too quickly and the passengers were thrown about in their seats. The bus had seatbelts fitted but not all the passengers wore them (the bus was designed as a fully seated bus). John now realised that he hadn't taken a break all day.

Before the next stage of the route, there was a steep hill. Road works had been going on below the hill for about a month. As the bus came down the hill, John took his foot off the accelerator and braked gently. He drove along a dual carriageway (built to motorway standard) at 120 km/h and was stopped by a Garda who asked to see John's documents. The Garda also asked for John's tachograph records. After inspection of the bus the Garda told John that his front near-side tyre was defective. This delayed John and his passengers, forcing him to wait at the roadside to have his tyre replaced.

During the conversation, the Garda also asked, "Did you check the bus before using it today?" John admitted that he had not done a complete check as he was in a hurry and forgot. The Garda then called a vehicle inspector who found more items that John would have found if he had conducted his walk-around check. The vehicle inspector also asked about the vehicle maintenance records and the fault reporting procedure at John's company. The bus was detained until the defects had been fixed. This was embarrassing and expensive for John and the company. John will now be prosecuted for negligence.

1

2

Case Study No.2

Alan had a full load of 70 passengers on board as he started out. His route was along the N-2 dual carriageway. While signalling left and slowing to make a tight left turn into St. Margaret's Road, which leads to the N-2, Alan noticed a cyclist in his left mirror. The cyclist was beginning to move up the left side (nearside) of the bus. Alan continued to watch his left mirror. He muttered to himself, recalling how the previous day he had encountered a cyclist wearing reflective clothing, riding on the left in a contra-flow bus lane. Alan noticed the cyclist glancing over his right shoulder. He usually had nothing against cyclists; in fact, he often went out of his way to double-check his mirrors and give them lots of room. He just wished he could give the careless ones a lesson or two. Alan heard a horn blow and a skid from a motorcycle approaching on his right side. The motorcyclist was warning Alan that the rear overhang of the bus had swung into the motorcycle's path.

Alan was agitated because of these events and, once around the corner, he tried to make up some time. He approached the next right hand corner a little fast, braking on the corner. He had to steer hard to avoid colliding with the kerb. Alan checked his mirror to make sure the passengers on the lower deck had recovered from the sharp turn. He failed, however, to check the passengers on the upper deck.

Once on the carriageway the drive went smoothly until the left front of the bus began to shake wildly and the steering wheel to vibrate. Before Alan could think the words "blow-out" his tyre burst. Taking a firm hold of the steering wheel, he carefully crossed two lanes of traffic to bring the bus to a stop on the right shoulder. A chunk of rubber slapped about inside the wheel arch as Alan brought the bus to a gentle stop. When the bus was completely stopped, Alan put on his high-visibility vest and told the passengers to please remain seated while he got off to check the situation. "Blown tyre for sure," he said while kicking what was left of the rubber. Before getting back on the bus, Alan displayed his warning triangle and tried to stop traffic by waving his arms. When he was unable to stop traffic, he got on the bus and turned on his hazard warning lights.

"We've had a blow-out," he explained to the passengers. "I'll contact my depot. In the meantime, please remain on the bus until another one arrives." No sooner had he contacted the depot than a passenger got up and moved toward the door. "Please, sir, you should remain on the bus. Another one will be here shortly," Alan said.

"I'm just going out for a smoke, if you don't mind," the passenger sniped.

"I'm afraid for safety reasons I'll have to ask you to stay on board, please. If you get off, others will want to do so as well and the traffic is moving at 100 km/h. Someone would surely get hurt," Alan replied.

The passenger stared briefly at Alan, then said, "Alright, I understand what you mean now," before moving back to his seat.

With this incident resolved, Alan quickly checked the passengers, making a mental note of the number of passengers (including children) and those needing special help. He contacted the depot again and reported the total number of passengers, including one in a wheelchair. After what seemed an eternity, a replacement bus pulled up and Alan directed the passengers onto the replacement bus. In the interest of safety and to save time, he loaded all of the luggage onto the replacement bus. He could tell this would be a long day.

1

2

Case Study No.3

Michael has been a PCV driver for many years. He is always professional in his approach to work and conducts vehicle checks (including plates) before taking charge of any vehicle. In his first job as a tour bus driver, Michael noticed that tourists carried a lot of luggage. He learned quickly how to stow and distribute luggage and pay attention to passenger limits. Fortunately, his employer was patient and took the time to explain things like stability, axle weight, the legal limits of each vehicle and the effects of overloading on tyre wear, braking power, and stopping distance.

Michael often travelled on bridges and roads that had a maximum gross weight limit to prevent damage. He knew that the weight difference between an empty bus and a full coach could be as much as 7 tonnes. Michael calculated the gross vehicle weight of his bus using the unladen weight and number of passengers plus an allowance for fuel, passengers, and luggage.

When planning a route, Michael considered the size of the bus. He knew the legal maximum width and length of the buses and coaches he drove as well as the swept area of each bus. In recent years, Michael had observed the introduction of different types of bus lanes. He always liked to get an early start so that he would arrive on time and could use the bus lanes that normally operated between 7:00 am and 7:00 pm. When the road was wet, Michael followed the 4-second rule, a point highlighted in TV road safety campaigns. He was particularly aware of this on motorways where vehicles were travelling at much higher speeds.

Michael's latest assignment involved driving a school bus for a private company for the school year. The bus had an emergency dry chemical fire extinguisher and a warning triangle but no other emergency equipment. It had proper internal lighting and was fully fitted with seatbelts. When necessary, Michael turned on the interior and exterior lights and he used the high intensity fog lights during low visibility.

Michael's bus was fitted with stability control and anti-lock braking (ABS) systems. One morning as he left, he noticed that his ABS light did not go out when the bus started or moved above 5 km/h. All the other lights on the systems warning panel worked normally.

It had begun to rain before Michael started work and it seemed the rain would continue for some time. He had planned his route. However, not far along the road there was a traffic hold-up and Gardai directed traffic onto a diversion route unfamiliar to Michael. On the diversion route, Michael had to deal with low trees, adverse cambers, cables, ESB poles, and some overhead obstructions such as shop blinds hanging over the edge of the road. Michael noticed a road sign giving the gross vehicle weight allowed on this road. Fortunately, this was more than the gross weight of his bus. Eventually, he rejoined his planned route and saw that the cause of the obstruction was a double-deck bus stuck under a railway bridge. The blue lights of the emergency services flashed hypnotically. Michael noticed in his interior mirror that a number of children on his bus were not wearing seatbelts and were standing in the aisle looking out the window.

As he waited for the hold-up to cleared and listened to the sound of the rain, Michael started to feel sleepy. He thought about his years as a PCV driver. During this time, he had seen the scale of private bus and coach services increase. He noticed that a lot of European coach operators were using tri-axle coaches. European Union regulations now governed international transport and the introduction of the euro had done away with currency exchange rate fluctuations. To qualify for international work, Michael would need a European Community licence and a bail bond. His employer would have to comply with international road transport rules.

Finally, the double-deck coach was cleared from the railway bridge and Michael could continue his journey. He looked forward to his next assignment as an international driver.

Case Study No.4

Sean began his route on a foggy, drizzly morning. He had not got much sleep the night before so he started his shift with a cup of coffee to stay awake and alert. He was in a hurry to start his shift so he rushed through the walk-around check of his vehicle (which was designed to carry standing passengers). He checked the mirrors, glass, brakes, wipers, heating ventilation, gearshift linkage, lights and indicators, tyres, engine oil level, reflectors, doors, and exit. Before starting the engine, Sean also carried out the following checks as part of his cockpit drill: mirrors, handbrake, gears, doors, and seatbelt. He did not think he had forgotten anything.

The figure below shows the items checked by Sean as part of his daily walk-around check and cockpit drill:

Sean's Walk-Around Check
Mirrors
Glass
Brakes
Wipers
Heating ventilation
Gearshift linkage
Lights and indicators
Tyres
Engine oil level
Reflectors
Doors and exits

Sean's Cockpit Drill
Mirrors
Handbrake
Gears
Door seatbelt

As he drove, several oncoming cars repeatedly flashed their headlights at the bus. Suddenly, realising his lights were not on, Sean turned them on full beam. There seemed to be more passengers at the stops this morning and, because of this, Sean worried about a possible time delay due to passengers boarding

At the next stop, Sean saw a passenger in a wheelchair with a large suitcase propped against the chair. He realised there would be a further delay due to picking up this passenger. Sean pulled up close to the kerb and helped the passenger onto the bus. When he bent over to pick up the suitcase, a sharp pain spread across his back. Unable to fully lift the suitcase, he slid it under the seat closest to the door.

Sean then asked the people who were crowded into the designated wheelchair space to move. An older gentleman with a cane refused to move, tapping his leg with his cane as reason to remain. Sean explained that the space was for wheelchairs and was not a designated handicap zone. He asked a group of seated passengers if one of them would please give up his or her seat for the gentleman with the cane. A young man smiled and obliged.

While Sean began fastening the straps that secure the wheelchair frame to the bus, the wheelchair passenger set the wheelchair brakes and also secured one of the straps. Sean double-checked the brakes and the strap the passenger had fastened. As Sean drove away, the young man who had given up his seat stumbled because he had not reached a new seat.

As the day progressed, the fog finally lifted. After Sean entered the motorway, he increased his speed to 70 km/h. His route took him from the motorway to a smaller road through a semi-industrial area. There were now more passengers than seats. Some of the standing passengers had become uncomfortable because the journey had slowed and there were fewer stops. As the bus travelled on, an articulated lorry sped around the bus, obviously too fast for the road. The lorry then turned left at a blind corner. Sean's route took the bus around the same blind turn. Once around the corner, Sean saw that the trailer had hit the bottom of a railroad bridge. To avoid delay, Sean quickly turned left onto an adjacent street, causing some standing passengers to fall into each other. Several passengers pointed out that this street was not on the route but Sean replied that he would still make their stops as he knew how to quickly get back onto the route. He decided to report the articulated lorry accident when he got back to the station as he was already running late.

One of the passengers became irate and demanded to get off the bus. Sean looked for a safe place to pull in. He saw yellow lines but there were no "No Parking" signs along the street so he pulled in and stopped. After the passenger got off, Sean turned off the engine and got out of the bus to do a quick inspection of the bus's exterior. Everything looked fine so he continued the journey.

1

2

Case Study No.5

Ciara drove a fully seated coach (with no standing capacity) between major cities. This was a kneeling-type coach, equipped with a hydraulic system which allowed the step level to be raised and lowered. Ciara was familiar with the system, its safe operation and secure storage of the equipment.

The picture below shows a ramp.

The picture below shows a lift.

Several elderly and special needs passengers depended on the coach service for mobility. If asked, Ciara helped these passengers. One passenger who was visually impaired often took the coach to visit friends in another city. This passenger needed help in finding an available seat. Ciara always used the kneeling facility for passengers who she thought it helped without being asked.

The picture below shows the type of cane that visually impaired people sometimes use as a mobility aid.

When Ciara picked up her visually impaired passenger this morning, she helped her to find a seat, stowed her luggage, and assumed that her destination was the same as usual.

Today was more eventful than most. At the beginning of the trip, Ciara discovered that there was an extra passenger on the bus. After a quick check, she found the unauthorised passenger and he got off the bus without incident.

During a brief comfort break (a toilet break), Ciara noticed someone in a hooded jacket open the luggage compartment of the bus and dig through the luggage. Luckily, a Garda was nearby. Ciara called the Garda over and she and the Garda approached the suspicious person who quickly turned around, obviously startled. He explained that he was a student looking for his book bag. Ciara quickly unloaded the luggage, stacking it in a pile to her side, until the book bag was visible. The Garda began to bring the student and his bag inside the building for questioning but Ciara indicated that it was probably an innocent mistake. She had seen the student's ID and had spoken briefly with him during the trip. The Garda insisted upon questioning the passenger.

When loading the luggage into the under-floor luggage lockers, Ciara placed the larger, heavier luggage in first. She remembered the unattended bag she had found on another trip earlier in the week. During a stop, she had brought this bag into the station and when no one claimed it, she left it with the ticketing agent.

Once back on the motorway, Ciara noticed that she was travelling at 90 km/h and changed her speed to match the speed limit. Since the luggage and passenger load were lighter than normal, she could tell the difference in the bus handling and found the accelerator and brakes to be more responsive than usual, especially when she was slowing or accelerating. On occasion, cross winds on exposed areas of the motorway rocked the coach. When leaving the motorway slip road, which turned sharply to the left on approach to the roundabout, luggage fell from the overhead luggage compartments. The previous week, when Ciara was driving a full bus around a sudden corner, some of the bags fell from the overhead compartment. Some passengers complained about the falling bags and said they had been jostled. Several passengers made a formal complaint about this incident.

Case Study No.6

Ashling was not familiar with the bus she drove today. She wondered how to find the information she needed about the dimensions, weights, seating capacity, maximum speed, and overhangs of the bus. She expected to have a full bus and so it would be particularly important to know the gross vehicle weight. Ashling was not sure how to calculate the gross vehicle weight. She had already checked the bus before she set out, checking the contents of the first aid kit and its location, the gauge on the fire extinguisher, the emergency hammers, and that the emergency exits were unlocked.

Ashling began her morning route thinking about the safety and comfort of the passengers. Her route contained several hills and she usually had a full bus.

Ashling had difficulty driving safely while trying to keep to her schedule. On downhill slopes, she tended to have trouble with braking. Sometimes the brakes overheated. Ashling was not sure how to use the hand-operated retarder correctly. As a result, she overused the foot brake. In addition, she failed to correctly use the "holding gears" (1, 2, 3 and so on) in the automatic gearbox fitted to her bus. She also took the corners too fast, causing passengers to complain.

The diagrams below show how forces in a moving vehicle affect passengers.

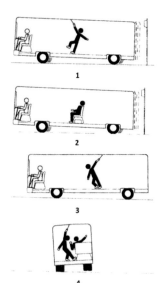

While turning left into a side road, Ashling correctly adopted a wider position farther out in her lane.

Driving along the new road, just past an arch bridge with a restriction sign, Ashling saw an older woman with a large piece of luggage. She stopped the bus for the passenger to board with her luggage. Ashling signalled and quickly moved off while the passenger was finding a seat. She heard a horn sound as she pulled away and noticed a motorcycle overtaking her. Ashling did not notice that the luggage was not stored. She was forced to brake hard, throwing the luggage along the aisle and injuring a passenger. Ashling made a right-hand turn into Barrow Street, a street with bollards at the entrance.

As Ashling built up speed, one of the passengers told her that smoke was coming from the rear of the bus. Ashling stopped the bus and opened the front door, which she remembered her instructor saying was the primary emergency exit. She told the passengers to get off the bus and directed them to a safe place. She then called the fire brigade. In pushing toward the door, some of the passengers fell. When the last passenger got off the bus, Ashling checked to make sure that all passengers were indeed off. She grabbed the fire extinguisher (required on all buses) and ran outside to find the source of the smoke. She knew that the smoke source would have to be found and corrected before the bus could continue its journey. She discovered that the smoke was coming from a tyre on the nearside rear axle.

The diagrams below show the bus's dimensions.

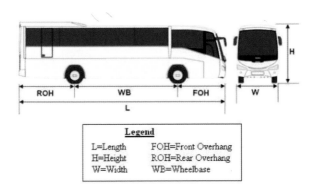

Legend

L=Length   FOH=Front Overhang
H=Height   ROH=Rear Overhang
W=Width   WB=Wheelbase